PAPER THONGS
& Other Misadventures

PAPER THONGS

& Other Misadventures

One man bares all

STEVE LEGG

CanaanPress

CanaanPress

Copyright © 2009 – Steve Legg

First published in Great Britain by Canaan Press in 2009

Canaan Press
PO Box 3070
Littlehampton
West Sussex
BN17 6WX
office@canaanpress.co.uk
www.canaanpress.co.uk

The book imprint of
Matt's Canaan Trust
www.mattscanaantrust.com

British Library Cataloguing in Publication Data
A record of this book is available from the British Library

ISBN: 978-0-9551816-6-5

Designed by Andy Ashdown
www.andyashdowndesign.co.uk

Cover photograph © iStockphoto.com

Manufactured in Malta by Gutenberg Press Limited

Dedication

To Rebekah.
You are one of God's
most amazing gifts to me.

Endorsements

I confess I have a vested interest – I like Steve Legg! And this book is like him. It is real in its response to the hilarious misadventures and the epic tragedies between which two extremes most of us try to walk a delicate balance. Steve, however, enters the extremes. The stories he tells are of a man who lives life to the full. Some things in this book will make you want to weep; others will give you a wry smile and occasionally ribald laughter. The book is like its author – entertaining, occasionally profound, and deeply human. Buy it and enjoy!

Eric Delve

Steve's stories are brave, funny and, like his most embarrassing one – leave a mark! We thoroughly recommend this book, especially to those of you who want quick access to challenging stories that may change your attitudes.

Lee & Baz

Steve and I have been close friends for more years than either of us care to remember. I have laughed uncontrollably at Steve's crazy antics; I have also been alongside him during painful and difficult experiences. In this book you will see a very human Steve, often in bizarre situations, but always totally passionate about sharing his love for God with others.

Ishmael

When you have a travelling ministry as Steve does, you gather more stories than most. Steve has, in his own unique way, told his stories and drawn out truths that will make you laugh, think and reflect. They are a challenge to people of all ages and walks of life. Get this book and give it to your friends – it's perfect to read over coffee, on the plane or in the other snatched moments in the busyness of life.

Norman Barnes

There's a saying in showbusiness – 'Only the truly great entertainers can hold an audience outdoors in Littlehampton when it's raining.' Well, coincidentally the last time I worked with Steve Legg was outdoors in Littlehampton and the weather wasn't great. He marched on that day with a kitchen utensil and a strait jacket and went down a storm during a storm. I've always admired people who are able to be entertaining and impart Christian truths without the clunk of, 'Uh-oh, here comes the serious bit'. Steve's great at that. He communicates without clunks. Enjoy this book. It's ideal reading material under your umbrella in Littlehampton.

Tim Vine

Steve is a unique bloke with a rare ability to cut through the rubbish and the clutter and speak straight to the heart. This is worth reading for the 'one way mirror' story alone, but there is so much more here than stories from over 20 years on the road with the great and the good. The insights are profound. You'll pause and think, you'll laugh, and you will definitely think afresh about life and faith. Read it and tell your mates about it. Nice one.

Carl Beech

Steve Legg is honest, candid and to the point and always inspires me to push on to be more creative and more proactive in my Christian faith. This book will indeed challenge you and inspire you to push on, but above all, it will bring you closer to Jesus and the clear reality that He always travels with us on our journeys through the ups and the downs.

Phil Collins

This is a delightful, at times humorous and yet serious book dealing with the issues of life. If you don't regard yourself as a serious reader, or if you are looking for something that is light, dip-in-able and yet carries a clear message – this collection is probably for you.

Gerald Coates

I have never seen a man get out of a strait jacket before and in under 60 seconds! Steve Legg is amazing. God certainly does move in mysterious ways.

Fern Britton

Steve's stories build into a roller-coaster ride of emotions, taking the reader from riotous peaks to tearful troughs. When the tears stop, he dries the eyes with a variety of comedic gems including my personal favourite – 'I don't need a car to look cool'. Yeah, right mate. I still maintain that it is in the daily life of Steve Legg, father, husband and friend, that his faith is revealed. For those that don't know Steve personally, the book provides a fascinating insight into his strange and wonderful world and a taste of the faith which inspires him to inspire others.

Tom Clark

This is the best book I've ever read. Steve Legg is a very clever man.

Mrs Legg – Steve's Mum

Acknowledgements

This book would never have had a life without the direction, help, encouragement and support of a select group of wonderful friends.

I am greatly indebted to Adrian Plass who suggested the book and the title, as we laughed and drank free coffee refills at Belfast International Airport – and missed our flight in the process. (You can read the entire saga on page 98.)

Thanks also to Eric Delve and Carl Beech for their wisdom and advice. Grateful appreciation goes to Lindy Leitch, Andrew and Daphne Taylor for their proof reading skills, and to the legend that is Alexa Tewkesbury for her copy-editing. She is an amazing talent and I am so chuffed to have discovered her. What a massive string to my bow she is.

Finally to Rebekah, my wife, what can I say? This would never have happened without you. Thanks for standing alongside me all the time. I am your biggest fan and love you so much.

CONTENTS

INTRODUCTION

I seem to have been blessed with an uncanny ability to get myself into embarrassing situations. Only the other day I managed to lean back, like Derek Trotter in *Only Fools And Horses*, and fall backwards into a cupboard. Later on, as I waited in the playground to pick up my kids from school, I was playing with a water pistol I happened to have in my pocket (as you do). One misdirected tweak of the trigger and there I was, in full view of all the mums, with a disconcerting wet patch on the front of my trousers. Then, when I got home, I walked straight into the patio door.

You see, however much I like to see myself as Mr Cool, sadly the evidence suggests otherwise.

In all the time I've known God, I've heard Him talk to me in many different ways. He speaks to me through His Word; through conversations with friends; through speakers at church and at other events; through the places I've travelled to and the experiences I've had – even through the untimely mishaps of my daily routines. And He speaks straight to my heart.

Through both the good times and the bad, I've been constantly aware of God's voice. I've watched Him at work in my life, and He's taught me some valuable lessons. Some of these have been learned the hard way, through struggle and heartache; others through sheer, out and out slog. This book offers a candid account of some of those insights, and the often bizarre situations God has chosen to use to teach them to me.

I hope you'll laugh a lot; I know you'll cringe just a little. And as you read of my antics and embarrassments, perhaps you'll be able to empathise in some small way with my struggles and misadventures, and hear God speaking to you through them, just as He has to me.

1

TRICKS AND TREATS

I do comedy magic. If you don't find it funny, it's just magic. Now, of course, it's not real magic, it's just tricks. I'd hate you to think I'm a witch and burn this book – especially so if you're flicking through it in a Christian bookshop. That would be terrible for trade.

My occupation does tend to raise a few eyebrows when I introduce myself to new people. Even my wife, Rebekah, laughed and answered, 'No, really, what do you do?' when she was first chatting me up. (If you stop reading for a second and listen hard enough you will hear her protesting across time and space that she never chatted me up – but as a man, I can assure you – she did.) She recovered admirably when I insisted that really, I am a magician and an evangelist, too. I use tricks and escapology to communicate the Good News of Jesus to young and old all over the country and beyond.

I've been performing for over 20 years and I love my job.

Standing on stage, telling people about Jesus and performing tricks are some of my favourite things. I'm passionate about communicating the Gospel in ways that people understand, in showing people that the Christian faith is relevant to their lives, and that being a Christian is not about wearing sandals (with socks, of course) and waving a tambourine (unless, of course, sandals and tambourines happen to be your own personal favourite thing). I love using tricks to demonstrate a point and laughter to help people listen. I consider myself truly blessed because every day I get to do what I enjoy most.

And I get to work with great characters, too. I've met and made friends with so many people who share the same passions as I do. Perhaps one of my greatest and longest-standing friends is the well-known singer, songwriter and author, Ishmael. He and I have performed together in hundreds of venues sharing with tens of thousands of people the message that Jesus loves them and wants to walk with them through their lives. We've shared good times and sad times and we've had more than a few laughs – many of them at my expense, although I'm sure Ishy would beg to differ.

One particular time, Ishmael and I were sharing the stage in a large, thousand-seater auditorium. Part of my act was to get a child up and ask them to give me one of their socks. I generally feel the need to make a comment about the smell and state of the sock, before placing it in my magic bag and asking the audience if they think I can turn the single sock into a pair. Of course, everyone knows that I can, so I put my hand into the bag and bring out a – *pear*. Pretty straightforward and very juvenile, but usually sufficient to raise some laughs and a round of applause.

Not this time, though. Ishmael had decided that he wanted to be the funny man – he had seen me do the same trick over and over again and he had tampered with my bag. This time, I called a young lad up onto the stage, was rude about his socks and played with the audience until I was finally ready to put my hand in the bag and announce as usual, 'Ladies and gentlemen, you all witnessed me put one sock into the bag, now here, as if by magic, I have a …' But instead of pulling out a pear as expected, I pulled out a … battery.

I was totally flabbergasted. The battery must have weighed the same as the pear and I hadn't noticed the switch at all. I yelled, 'Ishmael, I'm going to get you!' and ended up chasing him around the stage, which everyone found hysterical, and most probably thought was planned. It wasn't, and I was thrown just a bit, but the audience loved it.

Our lives can be like that – we can create routines, build traditions and make plans but things will come along and catch us off guard. Events break into our world and throw the plans out of the window, crashing through our routines as though they were made of nothing at all.

We like to protect ourselves with family and friends, with nice houses and cars. We work at careers and get insurance, but still things happen that are beyond our control. Good things and bad things – the daughter we've doted on brings home a boyfriend with a ring through his nose; illness comes; a beautiful woman appears just as we've settled happily into bachelordom; maybe we lose our job, or our spouse tells us they are leaving us for someone else – things that rock our world and shatter our dreams.

It can seem like the end of the world, but times like this can signal a new direction – exciting new opportunities to see what God has in store for us. The one thing we can be sure of when the goal posts seem to be moving around is that God knows exactly what is going on. Psalm 139 assures us that before we were born God knew every day we would live, and in Jeremiah 29 God reminds us: *'I know the plans I have for you – plans to prosper you and not to harm you'*.

When we align our lives with Him, when we give Him control of the plans, then we can relax in the knowledge that no matter what life throws at us, God is with us and will never leave us as He guides us on the adventure He has in mind. Instead of spending our time building fences around our neat little lives, let's sit back and watch to see what amazing surprises God has in store.

And never trust Ishmael with soft fruit.

2

A TOUCH CHILLI

Surrounded by the Word of God. That's a phrase I've heard preached from the pulpit more than once. Reading the Bible and filling ourselves with its wisdom is a good recipe for living a sound life. It's a message I thoroughly agree with and preach myself, but I saw the amusing side on one trip when I stayed with Mr and Mrs Smith, a couple who were members of the Gideon movement. (I haven't forgotten their name and replaced it with a generic one, they really were called Smith.) They very kindly put me up for the night after I performed in their Baptist church one cold Saturday evening.

Mrs Smith showed me to my bedroom – a charming little box room with a single bed, a flowery duvet, a dainty bedside lamp and the best part of 5000 New Testaments waiting to be given to hotels and schools around the country. I went to bed very literally 'surrounded'.

But Mr and Mrs Smith's house will stay in my memory for

more than this – and I may have stuck in their minds, too, for altogether different reasons.

Having returned the day before from a ten-day ministry trip in South Africa, I was jet-lagged and feeling the cold quite severely. When I arrived at their home, the lovely Mrs Smith turned down the volume on the snooker and said, 'Mr Smith, go and get this young man some salad, he must be famished.' I really didn't fancy cold salad one little bit; I wanted something warm and hearty, and quite frankly a little bit of grease wouldn't have gone amiss either.

Making my excuses, I headed out to the kebab shop I'd spotted round the corner. Never a one for going half measures I ordered an extra large doner with the works; lettuce, tomato, cucumber, coleslaw, garlic mayo and Thousand Island dressing, all smothered in Vindaloo-strength chilli sauce. I was young and single but the only reason any local girl would be falling for me that night would be because she was overcome by the sheer power of my breath.

Like a naughty little boy, I smuggled my kebab and bottle of lager past Mr and Mrs Smith – still both engrossed in the snooker – and into my bedroom and enjoyed my supper in record time, desperate to get to sleep. I was so tired I tumbled into bed before remembering that I was still wearing my contact lenses.

I dragged my tired body back up out of bed and into the bathroom. A combination of tiredness and maybe the beer made me lazy, but two seconds later I was more awake than I had been for days.

To be precise, for 'lazy', actually read 'didn't wash my hands first', and given that I had just been eating a kebab laden with industrial strength chilli sauce, this was fairly disastrous when taking out contact lenses. It felt as if someone had taken my eyeballs and dipped them in acid; the pain was unbelievable and all I could think of was stopping the fire in my eyes.

I splashed water on my face and stumbled round the bathroom with my eyes shut tight against the stabbing hot pokers that seemed to reach right into my head, and I grabbed what I thought was a towel. I wiped my face and eyes, groaning with relief as the soft fabric took the pain away.

As I opened my eyes, I groaned for a whole different reason. What I had actually wiped my face on was Mrs Smith's pristine white blouse which was hanging up next to the shower, ready for her to wear to harvest festival at church the following morning.

My ability to shame myself in other people's houses is quite unique, but I felt even I had surpassed myself on this sorry occasion. I made a feeble attempt to wash out the chilli stains and smooth away the many creases, before hanging the somewhat soiled Marks and Spencer top back on its hanger, and praying that dear Mrs Smith wouldn't notice. I then went and collapsed in bed again, surrounded by the Bibles, and slept like a baby until I sneaked out at 6:30 the next morning before Mrs Smith noticed the new pattern on her blouse.

The thing is, reading the Bible and immersing yourself in its wisdom is immeasurably valuable. But if you never put your brain in gear, it's like reading the entire works of Delia Smith but never entering the kitchen. We need to spend time reading God's Word, learning about our Father and His words of guidance for our lives, but then we need to apply what we have learnt, engage our common sense and walk with wisdom in the world.

Only slightly less importantly – always wash your hands before sticking your fingers in your eyes.

3

LOST IN TRANSLATION

Well travelled as I am, my ability to converse in anything other than my mother tongue is reprehensible. My grasp of foreign languages is a bit of a limp handshake – you could put all the words I know together in one line and it wouldn't make a sentence. Rebekah gets embarrassed when I ask for the English menu in a French restaurant. She helps the children practise asking for a coke with not just the right words, but a good accent, whilst their dad asks what beer they have in unashamed English.

I learned to be like this the hard way. I spent a couple of weeks in Paris with an evangelistic team doing street work in the heart of the city. I had been working with a translator for most of the week and had been listening intently to what she had been saying – trying to pick up some words here and there as she explained my escape from a strait jacket and talking about the Gospel. On the last day of our mission we upped the ante, and this time we asked two passing gendarmes to tie me up and verify that the jacket was indeed regulation.

I don't know about you, but I have always found the French police a little surly and lacking in humour, and I wanted to try and explain what we were doing – be friendly. All week I had listened to my translator, the lovely Anne, introducing me as *un virtuose d'évasion*. So, wanting to engage in some kind of conversation, I pointed at myself, tried to remember the terminology and said, '*Je suis un voyeur d'évasion.*' I've had some funny reactions to my choice of career in my time but this one took the biscuit.

Baffled by the concerned looks on the gendarmes' faces, I turned to Anne whose own face suggested that perhaps I had got something muddled up. Hadn't I just. Apparently, the all-important word I'd got wrong took me from being a professional escape artist to a peeping tom. I was a little concerned that getting out of a strait jacket might be the least of my problems.

My grasp of Russian proved even worse when I was having lunch in a pizza restaurant. The service was hardly silver and we waited two hours for our food to arrive. Arrive it did, though, brought to us by a surly waitress who looked like Christina Aguilera in a pink beret. Trying to exude patience I wasn't feeling, I smiled and said thank you as my plate was put in front of me. Except, of course – I didn't. Instead of saying '*spasibo*' as any self-respecting tourist would, I said, '*Srebrenitsa*', which is, as everyone knows, the Bosnian city which saw the biggest European massacre since World War Two. It was more heavy man threat than Christian graciousness.

Bizarrely, I may have made the situation a little better when later I left the restaurant and, keen to make up for my earlier genocidal mistake, made a final attempt to connect by saying goodbye. But again, instead of saying '*do svidanija*', I grinned from ear to ear and confidently shouted, '*Dostoyevsky.*' Great Russian theologian though he was, he wasn't really who I needed at that point. Still, at least 'Christina' would have realised that I was just a bumbling idiot, rather than a hit man sent round by the mafia to put the frighteners on.

Language is so vital. When communicating with people in other cultures, my translator is all-important – someone who can speak in words they understand. Sometimes, listening as a translator passes on something I have just said, I have been surprised by how long it seems to take, but I know that I may have used a cultural reference that makes no sense where I am, and they are taking the time to explain it more fully.

It's not just when we're abroad that we need to worry about whether we are understood. We need to think about the language we dress church up in, the words we use to talk about our Heavenly Dad. We take them for granted; we've grown up with them. The more we know, the better we fit in. But that means we can alienate people, too, because they haven't grown up with the words we are familiar with. They don't understand what we mean when we talk about atonement, redemption and sanctification.

In fact this is one of my bug bears – I am passionate about speaking in a language that people understand. It's why I started *The Son* newspaper – a tabloid that uses stories and language that anyone can connect with. It's so easy to make church a highbrow place where theologians and scholars are prized – but where does that leave most of us? Yes, we need to study the Bible – but the very word 'study' brings some people out in a rash.

We need to find ways to present God's Word that reach people where they are. We need to acknowledge that sitting and listening to a lecture style sermon for 40 minutes is far outside most people's everyday experience. People want to learn about God; the world is desperate to hear His voice. Let's make sure that, as He speaks through us, the message doesn't get lost in translation.

4

THE BEAUTIFUL GAME

It was May 1983 but I can remember it as if it was only yesterday. It was one of those days, filled with the promise of summer, the sun warming the ground from its winter slumber.

It was a year of new beginnings – compact discs were hitting the high streets, Alexander Graham Bell's grandson answered the first commercial mobile phone call, everyone owned a Rubik's Cube, and I'd had my first romantic moment, slow dancing to 'Every Breath You Take' by the Police at the school disco. *Flashdance* was the big hit movie at the cinema and girls were wearing crop tops and tight, stonewashed jeans set off with glitter coloured mascara. Happy days.

As for me, I was in the prime of my youth, about to leave schooldays behind me and step into the world of manhood. On this particular day I was in my element on the football field, playing in the Kingsleigh Secondary School Inter-Form Cup. The game had been long and exciting, with many twists and turns, and there had been a good few attempts on goal, but by the time the whistle went, we stood even at 1-1. There was nothing between us and victory but a penalty shootout and we had the best goalie in the school.

It was an epic battle and after five penalties each it was still stalemate. Now it was sudden death. The other team had scored and taken the lead. It was my turn to be a man, and step up to the penalty spot to keep our hopes and dreams alive.

Some 25 years later, I'm taken back to that balmy day on a school field in Bournemouth. I can still smell the freshly mown grass; can hear the girls cheering me on as I stood to take the final penalty to keep us in the game. Even my teacher was caught up in the excitement, chanting my name from the sidelines.

If I close my eyes, I can feel the adrenaline pumping through my veins as I licked my finger to judge the direction of the wind and balanced myself to take the vital shot. I can sense the firm connection with the ball as I blasted it towards the top right-hand corner of the goal. The sheer joy of living overwhelmed me as my hormones soared with the flight of the ball.

And I can still remember the sickness rising in my stomach at the sound of the ball reverberating off the post, and the horror as I opened my eyes to see it rebound and slam into the stomach of my form teacher instead of the net.

As bad moments go, this is up there in my hall of memories. I remember sinking dejectedly to my knees, as the other team ran around the field with their arms in the air, cheering. The girls, who previously were cheering for me, cast me a dirty look and ran to check I hadn't killed our tutor.

I went from being on the brink of manhood to a lost little boy in the space of three seconds. In years to come Pearce, Waddle, Incey, Batty and Southgate's misery after future World Cup and Euro shootouts would pale against my own personal trauma.

The isolation of the moment still comes to my mind every so often. That feeling of failure, of letting my team down, is still there as a memory over two decades later. The name of my teacher – Miss Saunders – is etched in my mind, as is the colour her face went as I winded her with my valiant attempt on goal.

So often we live in the shadow of past mistakes and regrets, never fully embracing the future and its promises. But God has promised us a new life where, although we may have to live with the consequences of the past, we don't have to live with the shame. *'Forget the former things; do not dwell on the past. See, I am doing a new thing!'* (Isaiah 43).

As we think about where we're going with our lives, let's not just concentrate on setting ourselves unattainable resolutions to run the London Marathon, have a six pack in two weeks and spend four hours in prayer every morning before daybreak.

Instead, let's resolve to stand out of the shadows that haunt us, to take hold of the promises that God has given us for a new life and walk into the amazing adventure that He has in store for us.

5

WHEN THINGS GO WRONG

One of the hardest things I have ever had to do is accept the failure of my first marriage. I was so determined that I should be able to make it work. So positive that I couldn't give up, couldn't lose my children and my wife – couldn't be a divorcee. I know there are countless people who have felt this, but as a Christian, and particularly as a full-time evangelist, I felt the pressure to succeed in my marriage even more keenly.

I bought every book on the shelves, from *Men Are From Mars, Being An Awesome Husband Volumes 1-5*, and *Marriage For Dummies*, right through to the classic, *Five Love Languages*. I tried to read myself into happiness and applied as much as I possibly could to my marriage. I felt that there must be something I could do that would fix things – if I just tried harder, listened more, bought more flowers, wore a different aftershave, stopped watching *Match of the Day*, tried to be more patient, or communicated in words of more than one syllable.

Ultimately, though, there wasn't anything I could do when my wife told me she'd had enough and asked me to leave. Short of handcuffing myself to the banister and refusing, which even I could see wasn't the answer, I just had to go.

It was one of the toughest times of my life. I was faced with the fact that I had lost my wife, my children, the house, the car, and possibly my job and even my dog. How could I carry on working as an evangelist when this news hit the grapevine? Who would still ask me to visit their church or their events when they knew that my wife and I were divorcing? How could God use me when I couldn't even make my wife happy? I felt like a complete and utter failure. A central part of my life – my bedrock, my home – had fallen apart and I didn't know how to carry on.

There were some people who said I shouldn't keep working. One of the leaders from my church came around and told me that I should step down and stop everything that I was doing because that would look better. One of my dearest friends told me that they could no longer have me on their team at events. It wasn't just me that felt I was a failure. There were plenty of others who felt that, because this part of my life had imploded, it meant that I couldn't carry on working for God. It was as though I was toxic and they were afraid I would contaminate others with my presence.

But there were others who walked alongside me; wonderful friends who invited me into their homes for coffee, or took me out for curry and a beer. Those who caught me walking the beach alone and asked me in to chat – gave me the time to talk through everything that was going on in my head. Perhaps most importantly, by their very invitation they were letting me know that they loved me and supported me and weren't afraid to be seen with me. They told me I should carry on. They told me that God had given me a gift and that I should use it. To stop, they said, would be to let the devil win.

It was very hard to know what to do. I didn't want to taint God's work with what was happening to me but I knew, deep down, that He is so much bigger than our personal circumstances.

In the end I just had to lay it all before God. No matter what else I had lost, He had stayed close by. And He has a remarkable way of cutting through the emotions and the confusion and speaking straight to our hearts. He even wrote me a letter.

It came in the post just five minutes after a church leader had walked out of my front door, having told me that he thought I should step down. Despondent, I sat at my kitchen table and opened my letters. The first one I read was from an organisation that had supported me for years. It enclosed a cheque for £20,000 towards *It's a Boy!*, the project I was working on at the time. The note with it read, 'We want to let you know that we support you in all that you are doing. You're doing a fantastic job. Keep going.' I got emotional all over again, but I got up, and I kept going.

Life throws some horrible things at us. Marriages do fail, loved ones die or betray us, illness comes and tears our world apart, jobs are lost, exams are failed and our children get caught up in situations that make us fear for them. There are times when moving forward seems impossible, when all we want to do is curl up in a corner and let the world carry on without us.

It seems as though we are not fit for the King that we serve and we have no idea how that can ever change.

The fact is, though, that none of us are fit for our King. That's the point. We are a broken and wounded people and it is only His grace that makes us whole. The Bible tells us that God's strength is made perfect in our weaknesses. The Gospels tell us time and time again that Jesus loved messed up people – He sought them out, made them whole and commissioned them to spread the News.

And right at the end of the Bible – there in the penultimate chapter of Revelation, God tells us, *'Behold I make all things new'*. There is nothing that can happen to us, nothing that we can do, that God can't turn into good. He is the Great Redeemer who can restore all things. When my wife first told me that she wanted out, I could no more have envisaged my life today than I could have scored a hat trick for Brighton at Wembley.

But God loved me amidst the mess that I was in. He stood by me as He stands by all who ask Him to. I found somewhere to live, I got my children back, and against all odds, I completed the *It's a Boy!* project. I continued to work in churches and take part in events around the country. I even fell in love again. Through it all I have discovered first hand that God is the God of second chances, and third, fourth and infinitum.

None of us are perfect; all of us have made mistakes and become tainted by the realities of life, but we have a God who washes us clean, who gives us His strength, His holiness, His grace and His work to do. We need to stand up when life knocks us down, take hold of His hand and go where He leads us.

6

CAUGHT SHORT

I have learnt to love hotels. I don't just mean lovely posh hotels with luxury quilts on the bed and baths big enough to swim in. Although they have their place, clearly they are more of a 'love at first sight'.

I mean Travelodges, Comfort Inns and other desolate buildings that call themselves a resting place for weary wanderers. It's not the thin blankets or the lumpy pillows; it's not even the fact that these days they don't even provide you with so much as a coffee sachet for the morning. No, it's the fact that they are anonymous and there is a far smaller chance that I will humiliate myself.

In a Travelodge, I can rock in when I want, nobody wants me to talk to them and I can order a takeaway which gets delivered to my room. I can also tune the TV to the channel of my choice which, for those of you who don't share a house with six women of varying ages is a rare and wondrous treat.

A Saturday night gig far from home has its disadvantages, but most of these are compensated for by the sheer delight of uninterrupted *Match of the Day*. One of the things I most appreciate, however, is that the bathroom is easy to be found. This may seem an unusual thing to value but by the time you have read this, you will understand why.

A few years back I was performing in a church in the north of England. I was accommodated by the lovely vicar and his wife. The journey up had been a good one – I seemed to have missed the worst hot spots for traffic and I'd had a clear run. The vicar and his wife were delightful – they had made me a hearty dinner, their youngest child had painted me a picture – even their teenage daughters gave me a smile. My hosts even insisted on giving me a lift to the church for the evening. They couldn't have been more hospitable.

The gig went well, too – I raised some laughs and more importantly children and teenagers came forward at the end to give their lives to God. A fantastic time, topped only by the vicar offering me a couple of glasses of wine afterwards. Everything was great. What a result.

Later I was shown to my room, which was a typical English vicarage treat. It's true that the décor was not quite what I would have chosen – rose and chintz – but I could appreciate the tastefulness and I certainly approved of the large, soft bed. I lay down, put my head against the downy pillows and sleep came swiftly.

The problem arose in the wee hours of the morning. And when I say wee hours I mean it in every sense of the phrase. It was pitch black and I was desperate for the toilet. I roused myself and got out of bed, opened the door to my room and stopped.

I definitely remembered being shown around the night before and I remembered the couple pointing out the bathroom. What I couldn't remember (this being the third house in as many nights on my travels) was which of the closed doors in front of me it was. I crossed my legs. It didn't matter how I went back over the tour, I just couldn't remember. I even went downstairs and tried to retrace my steps, but I just wasn't confident enough to try a door.

It was like one of the challenges on *The Crystal Maze* – pick the right door and you can relieve yourself of your burden, but pick the wrong one, wake the sleeping girl and you'll find yourself in more hot water than would fill a bath.

I went back to bed and tried to sleep. I lay on my front; I lay on my back and tried to think of England. But all I could think of was my ever-extending bladder. I had to go to the toilet. But I couldn't get it wrong and walk into a teenage girl's bedroom.

Finally, in desperation, I opened the window wide and went al fresco. I didn't know how loud water could seem when it plummets two floors and lands on a gravel driveway – I made Niagara Falls sound like a whisper in the wind. I would have frozen, but wasn't really in a position to do so mid-flow. Ladies, it is true – once a man opens the flood gates, he really can't stop. I just closed my eyes, thanked God that there wasn't a conservatory below and prayed for the end to come. It did, finally, and to my enormous relief, nobody came to see what the noise was, so I slunk back into bed, closed my eyes and waited for morning to arrive.

And this is why I love Travelodges. Not only is there a smaller number of doors to choose from – every hotel is the same; I could walk it in my sleep.

It may not have been a conventional solution to my problem, but it worked. Not that I recommend following my example in this. In fact my wife is somewhat ashamed I have shared it with you at all. But there are times in our lives when situations call for an unconventional solution. Sometimes we need to think outside of the box, if not out of the window.

Look at the guys who couldn't get their crippled mate to Jesus. They couldn't make it through the front door, but they didn't let that stop them. They climbed onto the roof, took it apart and dropped him down into the middle of a meeting, knowing that an encounter with Jesus would fix everything.

We can so easily fall into routines; we have tried and tested formulas for the things that we do – particularly as churches, but it's important to take time to step back, evaluate all that we do and be sure that there isn't a better solution. When we seem to hit a brick wall, it's time to start chipping away at the mortar and find our way through. Let's not get baffled by our problems or trapped in our routines. Instead let's open the window, enjoy the fresh air and take a new approach.

Just always check what's in the firing line.

7

MAD DOGS AND ENGLISHMEN

Back in the days before 'O' levels and work started to encroach on my life, when summer holidays seemed to stretch into an eternity of sand-filled hair and ice creams, I joined the Boys' Brigade. Drawn by the lure of football and the promise of joint activities with the Girls' Brigade, I signed up.

Our Boys' Brigade Company was affiliated to a church that was so dead it should have been buried years before, but I went along with my mates and enjoyed myself nonetheless. I was 13 and hadn't a worry in the world.

The summer of 1980 seemed to last from April to September, and in July we headed off to BB camp. Our mums packed our suitcases with a spare pair of pants, a toothbrush and some money for ice creams, and over 70 of us piled in the bus and headed down to sleepy Devon.

We stayed in Axmouth, a quaint little village with trams and a pretty harbour situated just down the road from Lyme Regis. It was idyllic and we spent all day hanging around our green ridge tents, listening to Blondie and Bad Manners on the radio, kicking a football, swimming in the sea – and playing pranks on our pals.

Keen to add some spice to the trip, some mates and I invented 'Axmouth Eddie' – an axe wielding maniac who scoured the town by day and night. Inspired by the Christian meetings we were having in the evenings, we told the younger boys that the only way to protect yourself was to wear the sign of the cross on your body, to ward off the evil man.

Sure enough, some masking tape was found and we all sellotaped a massive cross to our chests, oblivious to the stares from the other people on the beach.

One particularly hot day, my mate, Nigel Mason, proudly bearing his sticky cross, went off in search of an ice cream. Whilst he was gone, the group decided to head back to camp, so I picked up his bag and took it with us to keep it safe. Poor old Nigel spent half the day scouring the beach, first for his mates and then his bag, before realising that he had been deserted.

He finally turned up at camp hours later, wearing nothing but his swimming trunks, dehydrated and somewhat delirious, to find that, though we had barely noticed his absence, his arrival caused something of a stir. Bearing a striking resemblance to a lobster, we could feel the heat coming from him at 50 paces. Standing in his Speedos, he was swiftly slathered in calamine lotion, and it was painful to watch him wince as he gingerly pulled the tape from his chest.

It was quite a sight to behold. Nigel was going to be safe from Axmouth Eddie for weeks, if not months. There, emblazoned in purest white on his chest – from neck to navel, from nipple to nipple – was a huge cross, standing out against his crimson red skin. I was glad it wasn't me that night, trying to find a position in bed that didn't hurt.

But what I really remember from that week is the guy who led the evening sessions. He was a vicar called Bruce who played the accordion and told us about Jesus. Each night after supper, we sat in the big marquee singing songs about God and hearing how much He loved us. Bruce was a man who really knew God and who told us about Him in a way that brought Jesus to life.

Finally I had met someone who was excited about being a Christian, who explained that it meant more than going to church on Sunday and remembering to say grace before meal times. And at last I heard about a Father in Heaven who loved me so much He sent His Son to die on a cross for me – and this God wanted to be my friend.

I was awestruck, and it was here amongst the sunburn, the sea and the camaraderie of boys, that I asked Jesus to come into my life. Things have never been the same again. I, too, had a lasting impression of the cross on my life.

Coming from a family who didn't attend church, going to a youth group in a church which was barely breathing, this camp changed my life in a way that nothing else could have done. I am eternally grateful to the men and the one and only woman – the amazing camp cook, Miss Smith – who gave up their time to run it for us. Their sacrifice and commitment provided me and the other boys with a chance to encounter God and turn our lives around.

I know I'm not the only person who has had an experience like this – hundreds and thousands of young people are blessed year after year by attending camps and festivals organised by volunteers who love God and want to share that love with others. Others are touched because people have given up their time to run youth groups or after school clubs, or football clubs or film clubs – the list goes on.

My mother-in-law has run just such a group for over 20 years. I can't tell you how many precisely – I'd be in trouble, which is never a good move. Recently, a young lad from the local estate, who's been in more trouble than most, thanked her for what she's done. In fact he thanked her for 'spoiling' them when she threw a Christmas party and he asked her why she'd done it. Sometimes it's not the talks that we give or the shows we put on; it's not even the professionalism with which we do it – it's the love we demonstrate by doing it that makes the difference.

I am forever indebted to Bruce, Mr King, Mr Bradley and our other amazing Boys' Brigade leaders who gave up a week of their summer to share the love of God with me. I would urge all of us to find ways in which we can serve our community and give people a glimpse, through our sacrifice, of how God feels about them.

And I would advise campers everywhere, that going out in the noon day sun wearing nothing but a skimpy pair of Speedos and some sticky tape is not a good idea.

8

FRIGHT FLIGHT

Being 6'3" tall, flying really isn't my favourite thing. Folded up like a deck chair in cattle class, my limbs are usually screaming in pain before we've left the runway. Add to that the cardboard food, the toilets in a cupboard, crying babies and bad coffee and I've pretty much entered the world of nightmares.

Or so I thought before I truly entered a flying nightmare on an internal flight from Mexico City to Culiacan in the north-west of the country. I was travelling with my mate, Paul, to a 'Youth With A Mission' school and trying to cut costs. We had scoured the airlines and found one that seemed cheap but judging by the number of flights they offered, pretty popular.

My fears were first alerted on the journey to the airport when our Mexican translator, Martha, blanched when we told her who we were flying with. We enquired if there was a problem and she informed us that, cheap they may be, but Taesa airline had been having regulatory and maintenance problems for years since they had given up their nice new planes in favour of their cheaper-to-run, older versions.

Mexico City is not really the best airport to go to if you are feeling nervous about flying – it's hardly conducive to confidence. Set in the heart of the city, which itself is surrounded by mountains, it feels a little as though you are on some kind of suicide mission as you skim over the roofs of houses and hurtle straight towards the city's main road – the *Circuito Interior* – before taking an abrupt left and turning back towards the main terminal buildings.

The combination of the airport and the airline left me wondering if I might not prefer to walk the 650 miles to Culiacan. Nevertheless, I boarded the plane. The staff seemed courteous and efficient, which obviously doesn't guarantee that the wings are screwed on tightly, but I was taking my reassurance where I could find it.

This certainly wasn't from the pilot. He seemed to be the airline equivalent of a spotty teenager, who, having just passed his driving test takes his mum's Nissan Micra out for a spin with his mates, seeing if he can get it to go above 100 mph on a bend. Seriously, I thought I was going to die.

I know that take-off requires certain acceleration, but I think we could have gone into orbit with the speed we were doing. We hadn't even taxied to the runway and I was thrust back against my seat by the g-force. By the time we were actually heading down the runway I was gripping the armrest with a strength I didn't know I had, knuckles white, whimpering quietly. It was all I could do to stop myself from rocking back and forth and calling for my mum.

As we accelerated towards the *Circuito*, experience told me that we would turn right and join the runway proper, but, with the speed at which we were travelling, I was convinced that we were going to join the rush hour traffic instead.

Women were screaming and clutching rosary beads, men were crossing themselves and I almost expected to see a nun pull out a guitar and start singing 'Kum by Yah'. I'm not entirely sure my voice didn't join the screams as the pilot took the turn at such an alarming pace, we were thrown together by the centrifugal force. Without the seatbelts, I think we'd have all ended up out of the window and hanging on to the wing. As it was, the plane tilted so much that the tip of the wing brushed the dirt at the edge of the runway, leaving a trail in the dust to mark our passing.

My life had started to flash before me – all the things I had never done, the pretty girls I'd never kissed, the things I wished I'd said to my family before I'd left. I'd given up all hope of the nose ever actually lifting and taking us out of this improvised, aeronautical rally circuit.

But, up we rose eventually, and our terrifying airborne journey continued, only to have to make two more stops and horrific starts en route to our final destination in the north-west of Mexico. When I finally got off the plane, it took all the dignity that I had left within me not to get down on my knees and kiss the ground.

As the days passed at YWAM, we started to see the funny side of our aeronautical adventure and even to laugh about our ordeal, and it diminished in its severity. We returned to Mexico City on a comparatively boring flight and didn't think of it again until a week later – when we saw a news flash showing that the very same flight, Flight 725, had exploded in mid-air, killing everyone on board. It was a sobering moment.

In trying to cut costs, we had genuinely put ourselves at risk. As it turns out, we didn't get hurt (unless you count the wound to my pride at having screamed out quite so loudly), but it could have been very different. It wasn't necessary. So often in life we take short cuts and unnecessary risks. As Christians we put ourselves in dangerous situations when there is no need for us ever to be there.

I'm not talking about avoiding facing our fears, or sitting tight in our comfort zone, that's a different issue. I'm talking about inappropriate relationships, going shopping when we're not good with our money, hiring DVDs we wouldn't watch with our mum, or spending too much time with friends who encourage us to gossip. There will come a time when it is right to face these issues head on and conquer them, but we need to choose those moments carefully and know that we are doing it for the right reason.

We need to be wise with how we live our lives. We need to avoid things that will make us trip and fall, and we need to seek guidance from God through His Word and through friends we trust as we make our path in this world.

After all, scary plane stories are only good if you live to tell the tale.

9

OUT FOR A DUCK

I've been part of the team at Spring Harvest, a Christian conference held in a holiday camp at Easter time, for many years. In fact I've worked out that, after some 20 years, I have spent nearly nine months of my life living in a Butlins chalet.

Those of you familiar with the event will nod knowingly when I say that I can't be sure that I have ever actually seen the sun at this gathering. Spring Harvest wouldn't be Spring Harvest without relentless rain and a wind that threatens to bring down the big top. Perfect weather for ducks but your Bible tends to get wet.

Nevertheless, I've enjoyed many a wet week sharing a chalet with friends as we spread the Good News of Jesus with those who come to meet with God. There have been times of great blessing, times of deep teaching, times of awesome worship and times when, it may not surprise you by now to know, I have utterly embarrassed myself.

This particular week, I was sharing a chalet with my friends, Ishmael, Irene and Davy our drummer. Ishy has been my friend for longer than I care to remember. He was best man at my wedding and we have shared more curries than can be good for you.

We were leading the Family Celebration and had lots of great things planned. We arrived in the trademark Spring Harvest rain and trudged through the puddles to take our bags to our rooms. Davy only had the one bag so we left him in the chalet making sandwiches whilst we carried on unloading the car. By the time we returned, Davy had headed over to our venue to start setting up, and he had thoughtfully left the door ajar so as not to lock us out. After all, who needs security at a Christian conference?

Ishmael and I walked into the chalet, pushing the door open with our behinds because our hands were so full. I came in second and as I turned around, I saw him standing stock-still in the sitting-room – we had an intruder. Ishmael was facing up to a stray duck that had found its muddy way into our lounge.

It was one of the strangest moments – neither of us knew what to do. Caught up in the instant, I was barely breathing – tensing myself for the bird's first move. All three of us were paralysed in some kind of face-off, waiting to see who blinked first.

I came to my senses (briefly) and started to shush the duck out of the door in a gentle, mother duck kind of fashion. Clearly the duck felt it was more of a nasty Mr Fox manoeuvre and it took off, flying straight at Ishmael.

Ishy yelled, put his hands over his eyes like a child who still believes that if you can't see them, they can't see you, and fell behind the sofa. I screamed like a big girl and ran faster than Usain Bolt to my bedroom where I slammed the door (also like a girl) and then leant on it with both hands jammed up against the top to ward off the attack of the duck. It was like a scene from *The Birds*. I stayed like this for a good few minutes, breathing deeply as I recovered from my near duck experience, until it found its own way out, whilst Ishy and I cowered in fear.

There is not much pride to be salvaged from this situation. I utterly abandoned Ishmael. To be fair, it wasn't as if I left him in a room with an axe-wielding maniac, besides which he'd gone to the happy place behind his hands. At the end of the day however, I cannot get away from the fact that I ran and hid behind the bedroom door because a muddy duck quacked and flapped its wings at me.

I'm not even afraid of birds. That's the stupid thing. It just caught me unawares and I panicked. But I've had to live with the ribbing from Ishy ever since. As you might imagine, he has got a fair few miles out of that story (whilst never mentioning his own reaction, of course).

Fear has a nasty way of sneaking up on us when we least expect it. Just when we're at our most confident, just when we're about to take on a new project or make an important decision, it can strike right to our heart. It makes us want to run away and hide; to bar the door against the threat and stay inside where everything is familiar and comfortable.

If we let them, our fears can stop us from achieving our goals by disabling us just when we need to take action. We need to stand up and face them head on. It's not a weakness to feel afraid – Jesus did in the Garden of Gethsemane. He was so afraid in the face of His oncoming death that He sweated blood. But Jesus didn't run and hide; instead He felt the fear, looked it straight in the face and then gave Himself over to those who wished Him harm. What an awesome example.

When fears threaten to overwhelm us we need to remember that we don't stand against them alone. We have a God who has been there before us and who has promised never to leave us. With Him, we can stand, we can overcome our fears and we can go on to become all that we were meant to be.

But always keep an eye out for low-flying ducks.

10

A VISION IN BLUE

I met Rebekah on holiday. My kids and I have been going to *le Pas Opton* in France for years. It's a beautiful campsite on the West Coast run by Spring Harvest, and is somewhere we can really relax and enjoy ourselves; the kids love their clubs and I can read my book by the pool in the knowledge that they are safe. That year in particular, the view was enhanced by the foxy chick across the pool from me – a vision in a sky blue bikini.

When I first clapped eyes on my now wife, she was stretched out in the sun attempting to top up her tan, with a small blonde child lying on her tummy. With her free hand she was playing Ludo with her other daughter, and I was more than a little taken – particularly as it appeared that she was on holiday with her mum, and this was single parent family week. I myself had come away with my friends, Scott and Martine – Martine, in true form, took it upon herself to investigate further.

Judging by the puzzled look on Rebekah's face, Martine

was being subtle if odd, and soon reported back that there was no wedding ring to be seen. This was interesting news, though I was possibly more intrigued to see what kind of a tan line you end up with sunbathing with a little girl sleeping on top of you.

The week continued, however, without much to report. The children were happy, I was happy and the weather was good – all of us slowly turning into little brown berries. Maddie, my youngest, overcame her fear of the water and started to swim and I was king of the campsite barbecue – inviting friends and camping neighbours to share our burgers and sausages. But the blonde woman from across the pool remained elusive – she was a no-show at the single parent wine and cheese evening, so I satisfied myself with the wonderful spread that Care for the Family's, Robin and Cathy, had put on.

The debate continues as to who chatted up who. Rebekah claims that the whole Martine 'checking her out thing' renders the argument over before it's begun. I would disagree; I could no sooner have stopped Martine on a Cupid mission than stopped the sun rising or the tide from coming in.

Suffice to say that, on the last night of my holiday, at the bar, Rebekah chatted me up and I invited her to join our team in the quiz. We sat and nattered, exchanged phone numbers and agreed to meet up if I should ever be her way – which, it just so happened, I was going to be a fortnight later.

The rest really, is history; I spent a long time telling Rebekah that we lived too far apart to go out, but contacted her most days anyway. She, in return, told me that I was stupid thinking distance mattered but carried on chatting with me until the day that I realised she was right: I *was* stupid and distance only matters whilst you are apart. So I phoned her and asked her to marry me and solve the distance problem. It wasn't quite the proposal that every girl dreams of – down on one knee at the top of the Eiffel Tower, and I think it came as such a surprise she nearly dropped the phone – but it worked.

Rebekah was right. She often is, unfortunately. The thing is I had met the perfect woman for me, but all I could think of were the difficulties. She was, and is, everything I could ever want – beautiful, clever, funny, kind – and most importantly she loves God and she loves me and my four children.

And that's not an easy combination to find. Let's face it – it can be a big enough challenge finding someone who can love *you*, then as a Christian, you need to find someone who will love you *and* love God. As a single parent I was going for the triple whammy – love me, love God, love my kids. To be honest, I'd given up trying – I'd got my life working and was content with the way things were.

The Christian dating scene is a difficult place to be – I've heard women moan about the lack of eligible men, but I can vouch that, as a man, it sometimes seems as though it's the other way around. It's easy to question the biblical advice not to join yourself to someone who doesn't share your faith. I've heard lots of arguments around the topic and I've got friends who have dated girls who 'accept the beliefs' or who 'don't mind that they go to church'. I've got other friends who have gone out with girls, sure that they could convert them. I have to confess to having gone on a few dates myself with girls who didn't know God, something I wish I'd had the self-discipline to avoid.

It's a difficult thing, this not wanting to be alone, and there are a lot of wonderful people out there who don't know God – sometimes they are nicer than the ones who do. But I've come to look at it like this. There are two things in my life that are desperately important to me – my faith and my children. If I was looking for someone to share my life with, it was imperative that they should love my children, too, not just 'accept that I loved them' – it could never be enough for them to 'not mind *me* loving them'.

My wife would need to share my love for them; she would need to work with me to bring them up; she would need to help me in my relationship with them and help me to understand them more. She would need to encourage me when times with them are hard, and I would need to know that she loves to hear their stories and laugh at their ways with me. I would need her to understand that when one of them starts throwing up on Valentine's Day, then our candlelit dinner is going to have to be postponed because sometimes children throw our plans out of the window.

If this is how children affect my choice of partner, then it has to be the same for God. If He is important to me then I need to give Him the same priority in my life. It can never be enough to have someone tolerate your faith. They need to share it. They need to walk with you as you walk with God. They need to encourage you when you need it; they need to help you grow in your relationship with Him, help you to understand Him more, and they really do need to understand that God can disrupt our ordered lives even more outrageously than children.

Coming home from a gig and knowing that Rebekah wants

to hear how it went, having her pray with me before I go, knowing that she shares my passion for telling people about God's love for them, is something I treasure beyond words. She even has my little treats ready for when I get back in the early hours – a tube of Pringles and a can of nicely chilled John Smith's. This is real partnership; we're a team at home, with God and in our work.

Let's give God the importance that He deserves. Let's not compromise in the way we live our lives but instead choose to put ourselves in situations and relationships that will build our relationship with Him.

And if they look hot in a blue bikini, then that, surely, has to be a massive bonus.

11

KNOW IT ALL

My youngest daughter, Megan, is still at the age where she asks questions endlessly. She thinks about things and wants to know everything. She wants to know how everything works, why everything works, what we would do if it didn't work and then she wants to go to the factory to see it being made. So far, on our list of exciting places that Meggie wants to visit, we have a pencil factory, a glass factory and somewhere that makes televisions.

Recently on one of those long road trips destined to drive parents to distraction, I had mislaid my copy of *Now That's What I Call Ishmael 43*, so the children were listening to the adventures of *Psalty The Singing Song Book*. If the long drive doesn't send you mad, the CD will.

Psalty does exactly what he says on the tin and goes around teaching very American children – and mine as they listen in – all about Jesus. This particular episode had seen a little booklet (don't ask) called Melody, choose to follow the Lord and she had prayed to ask Jesus to come into her heart. Megan was looking thoughtful – for a while she just sat quietly in the back of the car whilst Psalty and the kids sang, 'I've Got That Joy, Joy, Joy, Down In My Heart'.

Never a one to expect quiet to last long, I wasn't surprised when Meg piped up with her thoughts which went something like this –

'Mummy?'

'Yes, darling.' (This is my wife, of course, I don't generally answer to Mummy.)

'Mummy, when we are friends with Jesus, that means He comes to live in our heart like He did with Melody?'

'That's right, sweetheart.'

Megan looked thoughtful and we waited:

'Don't you think He'd have more to eat if He lived in our stomach?'

What do you say to a four-year-old? Later, on the same journey, she had a worried face and more questions –

'Mummy?'

'Yes?' (It's great when these difficult issues get directed at my wife.)

'If Jesus is our friend, that means He goes everywhere with us, doesn't it?'

'Yes, darling, He does.'

'So He's in the car with us now?'

'Yes, Meg, He never leaves us.'

'Do you think He's remembered His seatbelt – 'cos I wouldn't want Him to get hurt?'

Children see things in an amazing way. They are literal beings who cut through the nonsense and see things for what they are. And they make me laugh. A lot.

They also make me think. Just the other day Megan was off on another verbal adventure – exploring the world around her. Our rabbit, Ringo, had just died and she was very concerned about the fact that we hadn't been able to bury him because the ground was frozen solid. We moved through what happens to rabbits when they die, and came around to what happens to people.

Meggie wanted to know how we go from being in the ground to being in heaven. We tried to explain that we will have new bodies but the questions just kept coming. How will we find them? How will we know which one is ours? How will I know who you are if you look different? It got to the point where I had to hold my hands up and say that I just don't know, but I know God has got it all under control. Megan looked at me as though I had just told her that there's no tooth fairy and said, 'But, Daddy, you know everything.'

But I don't, and I have to accept that, even though that can be really hard. I have friends who have left their faith because they can't find all the answers, because they don't know precisely how God made the world, because they can't fully get their head around the Trinity, because they don't know what's going to happen at the end of time or when that's going to be. I sometimes think that when Jesus said it is easier for a camel to go through the eye of a needle than for a rich man to enter the kingdom of God, He could have added an intellectual man into the script.

In our intellectual pride it is easy to think that we must understand everything. But what kind of foolishness imagines that it can fully understand the Creator of the universe – the Lord of heaven and earth? God is greater than all we can ever imagine. We should never try to shrink Him to fit into our understanding.

Instead, let's worship God in all His wonder, in all His glory and mystery. Let's marvel that this God who created the universe should want to be our friend. Let's spend our lives seeking to know Him more, in the knowledge that one day we will get our own private audience, when we can be like Megan and ask our Heavenly Father all the things we've ever wanted to know.

And there will be all the time in the world to listen to the answers.

12

TAN-TASTIC

I write this chapter very nervously – overwhelmed by an acute sense of embarrassment and humiliation.

If nothing else, please admire my bravery because this is not an easy one to admit publicly ... Last summer I had an all over, spray-on, San Tropez fake tan.

Please understand I did this ONLY as a favour. I'm a regular at the local gym and a pal of the boss, who was desperate for a bloke to be sprayed in the name of staff training for this new piece of equipment. I was also conveniently going to be appearing on TV the next day, but vanity, of course, had nothing to do with my decision to undergo this particular beauty treatment.

So there I stood in a booth wearing just pants (I drew the line at a paper thong) being sprayed by the expert – a large lady from Essex – while a team of beauticians from the gym stood and watched.

Performing and speaking at dozens of outdoor events each summer, I usually have a pretty good tan anyway, but never had I looked so brown. I made Dale Winton and David Dickinson look positively anaemic. I was now a perfect shade of mahogany. So were the pristine white sheets that I slept in whilst visiting friends that very same evening.

I woke up, and as a member of the 'new man club', went to make my bed before realising, horrified, that I'd left a little bit of myself behind as a memento – the bed sheets could have been mistaken for the Turin Shroud.

It even crossed my mind that I could have sold the sheets on eBay as artifacts from a time gone by. I had more than left my mark, and was forced to explain to my hosts, in case they should think that they had given hospitality to a man with a strong aversion to showers – I was more than a little embarrassed.

But it made me think. As Jesus' followers, we *should* leave a mark – not a dirty stain that betrays our attempts to change how we look, but mementos of our true identity in Christ.

As salt and light we are called to make a difference; in our conversations in the gym, our negotiations in the office, with the boys at the pub, the way we speak to the person who clearly knows nothing on the other end of a helpline, and in the way we cope with squabbling children when we come home at the end of a long and tiring day.

Everywhere we go we leave a mark of one sort or another and we sometimes inadvertently have a profound effect on the people we encounter. In all this we are ambassadors for an almighty God, and it is His mark that I for one, want to leave behind with the people I meet.

13

OBSESSIVE? — MOI?

My son can spend hours on his Xbox. Playing football and war games with friends online, he whiles away endless time sitting in his bedroom oblivious to the real world going on around him. I don't like it. It makes me worry that we're raising a geek.

We limit the hours that he spends on his computer and insist he takes real time out with his physical family, but I fret about the change that has come over him – he has gone from a boy who played football until the sun went down, to a child with one hand on his game controller and the other typing messages to his mates on MSN, whilst his vitamin D levels diminish before our very eyes.

I don't know where he gets it from. Well, I didn't until my wife pointed out that I am a bit of a closet geek myself. I don't like this thought, preferring to see myself as a man's man. But it's made me think.

Like most men, I have to confess I love gadgets. All of them. I'm a total sucker for a little thing that can do a job that I already do perfectly well by myself. I subscribe to a gadget magazine – full of the latest bits and bobs to fill your drawers and satisfy your masculinity. I love it, and if something is electrical, too, there is an extra thrill. I don't have matches to light the birthday candles, I have a flame throwing lighter that half melts the candle before actually igniting it, but boy do I feel like a real man using it.

Don't even get me started on Sat Navs – I use mine to get me to Tesco. In fact I actually have two Sat Navs currently in my car – the built-in one that came with it, and a peach of a Garmin model that I was sent to review for *Sorted* men's magazine. Speaking of which – what a dream that is. Having started *Sorted* over a year ago now, I'm proud of all of it – the interviews, the reviews, the advice on faith and fitness – but really, the bit that I get down to first each month is the gadgets page.

I love my iPod and have spent hours pouring over my pc downloading little snippets of comedians, and pod casts from shows I enjoy, compiling a digital collection of audio heaven.

Most recently we went to dinner with some friends and I saw that they had a marine aquarium screen saver. I raced home after a lovely meal and before midnight I, too, had one, and had even chosen my fish – the thrill of the digital world.

My wife, whilst generally bewildered by my excitement over such things and unimpressed when I stay up to the wee hours adjusting my virtual fish tank, surprised me with an eReader for Christmas. I can't tell you how much more pleasure there is to be got out of digital books than real ones.

The satisfaction of loading books onto this electrical marvel is immense. I may even read them.

And then there's my phone – it's hard to explain the sheer joy it brings me with its Internet and email capabilities. I have to confess that I was nearly late for my own honeymoon because the latest BlackBerry came out the day after my wedding and I scheduled in a visit to the phone shop to collect it en route to the airport.

I then spent hours assigning ring tones to friends and family so that I know, even before I look, who is calling me. I've downloaded the theme tune to *Wonder Woman* for Lindy, my amazing publisher, *Danger Mouse* for my son, Jay, and *Happy Days* for my wife. (The happy days nearly came to an end so I hastily turned the phone off for the rest of the honeymoon like a man who knows what's good for him.) My particular favourite is the tone I downloaded for my incoming texts – a rip roaring wolf whistle – you can't miss it, it's great. Got me into trouble, but that's a whole different story.

The gadgets themselves, though, great as they are, can become a bit of an obsession. Complaining about my son being anti-social is akin to the man pointing out the speck in his friend's eye whilst leaving a log in his own. Lying next to my wife by the pool on holiday, with my iPod in and my eReader on, hardly makes me the life and soul of the party – as I discovered when I finally looked up from my virtual book and realised Rebekah had gone in search of someone who would talk to her.

It's not just gadgets, we all get obsessed by things – a project at work, keeping the house clean, going to the gym, following our football club, developing the garden, knowing the latest scores in the cricket or maybe even getting involved at church. All of these things are noble pursuits when kept in perspective, but if we let them crowd in, they can push out the things that are really important to us – the people that we love.

The people around us need our time. They need us to put aside the distractions that we love, to listen to them and give them our undivided attention. We need to prioritise building the relationships that we have – take our son to see the football, play a game with our kids, take our mum out for coffee, our mate for a pint and our spouses out to dinner.

After all, with the wonders of i-Player you can always watch *Match of the Day* later in peace.

14

DIRTY DANCING

Following my disturbing revelations earlier in this book, it has been bothering me that there are more. Truth be told, I am slowly but surely stacking up a list of truly embarrassing gym moments that are making it harder and harder to show my face in the changing room.

It's not my face, though, that's been creating the problem – it's my pants. You may remember that prior to giving my body – in the name of beauty – a St Tropez all-over fake tan, I was told to strip and put on a paper thong, but there was no way I was doing that.

I wouldn't wear a paper thong for anyone. Instead, I thought, I would prefer to wear my own, more manly boxers … Until, that is, I realised I had a small, wet patch on the front. The men will know what I'm talking about – a moment of haste in the bathroom – an hour of damp in the pants.

Never one to want to show myself up in front of a lady, not

even a large lady beautician from Essex, I set to fixing the problem. Stopping to check that no one was around I positioned myself in front of the hand driers and got the hot air blowing. Picture the scene – me, a fully grown, 6'3" man, on my tip toes, gyrating around in my pants in front of a hand drier. It's not hard to imagine – I know this, because every time my wife tries, she ends up on the floor in hysterics.

And of course, just as I am working out which of the differently positioned hand driers has the best angle, two men walked in and stopped dead in their tracks behind me. There was nothing to be said. I just turned and tiptoed off to my tan.

Secrets, embarrassing moments, things we think only we know, have a horrible way of finding us out. I'm not just talking about being caught out by a couple of guys who were probably more traumatised than I was by a silly event in the gym. I'm talking about the dark thoughts we harbour, the pictures we entertain in our minds, maybe even store on our PCs. We may never get physically caught out. But those images, those thoughts, the unkind wishes and the selfish moments – they eat into our soul and permeate everything we do until the selfish thought manifests itself in a selfish action, and the pictures lead us to dishonour those most precious to us.

God sees right into our hearts, and He wants to wash them clean. Let's not keep allowing the mess back. Let's stop the thoughts when they start, delete the images without looking at them, practise looking for the best in others, and let these be the seeds of our actions.

And never, ever think someone won't walk in when you're dirty dancing in front of a hot air blower.

15

ANGELS WITH DIRTY FACES

It was a gloriously sunny day as we approached a Roma Gypsy camp in downtown Belgrade. The Romas are a forgotten people – well, perhaps forgotten is not quite the right word, but they are certainly out of sight and out of mind. During the communist era, for the purpose of control, Roma communities were settled in areas on the outskirts of towns or other unpopulated areas where they wouldn't be in the way.

This is where you will find most Romany people today – inhabiting these 'ghettos' with no running water, no electricity and no sewage system. The obvious consequences of living in such conditions is a general lack of hygiene that means children are socially excluded at school, adults are refused treatment in hospitals and find it almost impossible to gain employment. They are caught in a vicious circle of illiteracy, poverty and joblessness.

But this was where we were heading. I was travelling with Samaritans Purse, and we were working on their Operation Christmas Child campaign. For months, churches, schools and businesses had been filling shoeboxes with presents – toys, colouring pens, hats, scarves, toiletries and hair bands. Samaritans Purse receives tens of thousands of parcels and distributes them around the world to children living in poverty who would otherwise receive nothing at that special time of year.

Our minibus drove up a dirt track reaching the underside of a bridge that had survived the NATO bombings a decade earlier. This was home to angels with dirty faces – two acres of ramshackle living quarters, rubbish dumps, lines of dingy laundry and unfriendly dogs. But our visit meant that Christmas had come early for 300 wonderful, wonderful children. They all looked younger than they probably were but their dirty faces, complete with matted hair and runny noses, were wreathed in smiles.

I took my bag of tricks from the van and started to entertain the crowds who had gathered for hours before our arrival. They, very encouragingly, cheered and laughed in all the right places, and at the end of my show I explained how God loved them and thought they were very special. A young mum holding a couple of children shouted back in her stilted English, 'Thank you very much,' and the cheering reached a crescendo.

Now it was time for the presents ... and more cheers. Eventually over 300 precious children went back to their homes with shoe boxes full of goodies.

There was a little girl, Tanja, the same age as my ten-year-old daughter back home, and she has remained in my memory.

I was incredibly touched when she opened her box containing her only Christmas presents that year; she loved the pencil box, the doll and the plastic jewellery, and paraded proudly through the muddy tracks in her dirty old shoes wearing her plastic 'bling'. Little things, cheap things that children in our own families might look past for their real presents, but they were treasures beyond measure to her. This is what Christmas is really all about.

For hundreds of children a little bit of heaven came to earth that day. The value of those gifts didn't lie in the amount of money that had been spent. It didn't even matter that some of the items were second hand or donations from a child who had more toys than they knew what to do with. The worth of those gifts was that those children, on that day, knew that they weren't forgotten, that they mattered to the person who had spent time filling the shoebox and that they were of endless worth to the God who created them.

Simple things like this make such a huge difference. Filling a shoebox is such an easy thing to do – it's a fun afternoon out with our children that costs just a couple of quid, but it can change the life of someone you may never even meet.

In Matthew's Gospel, Jesus explains that when we feed, clothe or visit those who are overlooked or ignored then it is as if we did it for Him. We need to seek out these opportunities, not just sit in our comfortable homes. We need to go out looking for people to help but we don't need to go far. We don't have to catch a flight to find individuals who are lonely or in need; they live in our country, in our city, maybe even in our street.

We don't have to make grand gestures either. I recently had

a conversation with Sybil who works behind the till at Iceland. We got talking about her favourite treat – a fresh cream apple turnover from Regency Patisserie in our village. I paid for my shopping and headed straight there. Sybil's face when I returned with her cake was priceless.

Simple things; a bottle of wine, an offer to baby-sit, a lift to the shops, a remembered birthday, half an hour of our time shared over a cup of coffee is all it takes to show someone that you have thought of them and that they matter to you. And as they learn that they matter to you, it will get easier for them to understand their endless worth to God.

16

IT'S A MAN'S WORLD

In our house I like to think that we have a pretty fair division of labour. Having brought up four kids by myself for five years, I've learned the mysteries of the washing machine, I have overcome the fear of an iron and I actually quite enjoy cooking – my roast potatoes are legendary.

I have to admit, though, that when I remarried and Rebekah and her children moved in, I sat back and enjoyed the energy that she displayed for keeping the house clean and tidy and marvelled at how white she could get the clothes. But I still do my bit – we take it in turns cooking and washing up, I make the bed and under instruction I load the washing machine. Occasionally I even offer to do some ironing, albeit in the full knowledge that Rebekah will say no because she is unable to bear the pain of watching me take half an hour to do what would take her five minutes.

But there is a time when I come into my own – a whole

season when I become the provider. Summer time is barbecue time and this is totally my territory. Talk about gadgets, my barbecue is the king of all barbecues – a four burner, hot plated, steel hooded beast on which I could cook a whole cow. I love it and cherish it and brush it with oil, and I'm saving up to get the ultimate add-on rotisserie.

Each year we have the grand unveiling of the barbecue as soon as it is vaguely warm enough. To be honest there just needs to be no snow on the ground. I've been known to have barbies in January. We invite the neighbours round to share in the occasion and there I stand, lord of my domain, turning the sausages and frying the onions. It gets better than that – I make a mean minted shoulder of lamb and love to sear that on the coals before grilling it till it drips with juice. For dessert I grill mango and melt bananas with chocolate, a culinary delight that has to be tasted to be believed.

And I do it all myself. It's not that I don't trust Rebekah, but it's my job. It's my job in our house, and I prefer to take over at other people's houses, too. A man's place is by the barbecue with a monstrous pair of tongs in one hand and a chilled can of Fosters in the other; in charge of the grilling to save him having to engage in chit chat with people he doesn't know.

This was all very well until I promised the children a barbecue at the weekend forgetting that I was going to be away doing a gig in the north of the country.

My wife was going to have to take control of my barbecue. We both felt pretty uncomfortable at this blurring of our territories. I came over cold and sweaty at the thought of Rebekah touching my utensils and she suddenly realised that she didn't even know how to turn the beast on. We had to have some swift staff training and it was with great trepidation that she took over my mantle.

I hate to say it, but she did a good job. I came back and checked, of course, asking the kids if Mum's sausages were as good as Dad's to which they gallingly sang a resounding 'yes'. Moreover, she got cocky and created home-made burgers which the kids were raving about. I felt a little redundant. After all, the reality is that for our regular barbecue Thursdays, Rebekah already does a fair chunk of the work – she buys the food, prepares the salads, bread, utensils, napkins, sauces, lays the table, marinades the meat and clears up afterwards. Whilst I clearly have the most important job – standing over the barbecue … I'd been emasculated.

It's not just barbecues. There are all kinds of things in life where we take our hold and make the role our own. It happens easily and often there's no option, but we need to make sure that we're not the only people who can do what we do. It is so easy to get caught up in a role, imagining we're the only one who can do it. It's simpler to do something ourselves than go through the hassle of teaching someone else and then watch them do it badly. And sometimes it's tempting to keep it to ourselves because it makes us important, keeps us useful and makes people need us.

One of my dear friends, Norman Barnes, has said to me many times, 'You need to be bringing up your replacement, mentoring someone younger.' He's not talking about my skills with a spatula and some hot coals, he's talking about my ministry, and I know I'm not the only person he says it to.

We need to be training the generation of the future, not just to be church leaders but in other ways, too. One of the things I love about my blokes' magazine, *Sorted*, is the opportunities it has given me to get people involved who have never written for something like this before. I've had to take steps out into the darkness sometimes, trusting that what they provide me with will be good enough, but they've never let me down yet, and unless I encourage and mentor these young writers, how will they develop their skills?

Jesus modelled mentorship – not just with one person but with 12. He spent real time with His disciples helping them to grow and develop their skills, so that when He left earth, they could carry on His work. Interestingly, He didn't expect them to be exactly the same as He was – that was unrealistic – but He encouraged them in their different gifts to take His message to the world, and what a job they did.

So let's not hold on to our positions in life and get precious about who we entrust things to. Let's encourage those around us to get involved, share our passions with people who care, and mentor men and women to carry on the work.

After all, if they do the work, there's more time for the barbecue.

17

INSTRUCTIONS ARE FOR WIMPS

DIY and I have a strange relationship: as a man I feel the pressure to be able to put up shelves, hang pictures and lay a patio without breaking a sweat. It's one of those man things – where your masculinity rises by the number of power tools in your shed and your testosterone levels are directly linked to the speed at which you can pull a Phillips screwdriver from its holster on your tool belt.

Beyond this – the pinnacle of manliness is surely to be found when you don't even need to read the instructions; when, without so much as referring to a guide, you instinctively know how to lay the struts for the decking and where to position the footings.

But the reality is, I would much rather pay another man to come and do the jobs for me because, you see, I'm just terrible at DIY. I once heard my wife telling a friend that when it came to DIY I did the job of two men … Laurel and Hardy.

I just don't like it. I don't want to prune the hedges; I don't want to mow the lawn. I don't want to paint the ceiling and I don't want to spend all day trying to get a shelf straight. I don't even want to understand how my boiler works, let alone be able to fix it. Between you and me, I wouldn't change a light bulb unless it was the last in the room to go and I wanted to read in the middle of the night.

In fact there are a lot of things I'd rather do than DIY, which is why when my garden fence started to look in need of a lick of paint I picked up a copy of the *Yellow Pages*. All set to phone a chap and get him to do the job for me whilst I got on with something more interesting, I flicked to the handyman section, only to find a list for 'Dial a Hubby', 'Husbands 'r' Us' and 'Want a Man?' I felt a little disturbed. I was sure I didn't want a hubby and now I was beginning to doubt my manhood. There was nothing for it; I was going to have to paint the fence myself.

Having psyched myself up for the job, I went with my oldest daughter, Amber, to the hardware shop. Hardware – what a masculine term; it makes you walk taller just reading the sign. Armed with enough knowledge to fill a matchbox, we chose a colour for the fence paint (green because it makes your garden look bigger – that's a special Steve Legg DIY fact) and were starting to look at the brushes, when my eye caught sight of the special Power Sprayer for the aforesaid paint. Now there's a tool to store in your shed.

More to the point, it said you could spray 12 fence panels in less than 30 minutes. Excellent, I was going to have all the kudos of being a DIY expert and owning a new power tool, and any hard work would be over by elevenses.

I got home, changed into my man clothes and went out into the garden. Amber came out to watch her dad as he went about his man tasks. My chest puffed just a little, with pride, as I displayed my man abilities to her, basking in the confidence that all little girls have in their dads.

I filled the tank with paint, turned on the power and watched as the pressure rose in the machine. A minute later, you could still hear the power of the machine but nothing seemed to be coming out of the nozzle. Not wanting to diminish myself in my daughter's eyes, I took a closer look. With relief I realised that the nozzle twisted to adjust the spray and it was currently turned off.

Glancing at my daughter, I gave her a confident smile before turning back to the nozzle and giving it a twist. In my manliness I had indeed worked the machine out. Paint came powering out of the hose and straight into my face as I stared, hypnotised at the nozzle. In 15 seconds flat I was covered from top to toe in ten litres of forest green *Cuprinol*. My hair was green, my clothes were green; it had even got in my eyes where it had come out of the machine faster than I could blink. I was crying green tears. My daughter was crying too – with laughter.

Had I read the instructions, I would have been warned of the folly of looking at the nozzle with the machine turned on. I would even have been instructed to wear eye protection. More fittingly still, I would have been told to '*use your common sense*'. If only I could find it.

In my haste to impress, in my need to prove myself to an eight-year-old and perhaps to myself, I failed to read the manual. It's so easy to do. So easy to think you know best, that there's nothing you can be told.

The Bible is full of wisdom, pithy anecdotes and sage advice. It has cautionary tales and words of warning. But we don't take the time to read it before we blast into our day and set about our tasks. How many mistakes could we avert? How many tears could we save if we determined to read the Maker's Manual before we tried to do things our way?

18

IT'S GOOD TO TALK

My wife can talk. For hours. Seemingly without stopping to breathe at times. She can while away eons to her friends and family on the phone. She even talks in her sleep. She has an astounding ability to find things to say in all situations to all people. And if she hasn't got anything to say (a rare and worrying occurrence) she asks questions – lots of them.

I, on the other hand, have been referred to as a man of few words. Of course, on stage I'm the life and soul of the party and don't stop, but like many entertainers, privately, I'm not so forthcoming. In fact when I met my wife I made a big point of letting her know that I can't talk.

I think I may also have mentioned that this made me bad boyfriend material which, of course, in true female fashion she decided was me being commitment-phobic and chose to ignore. However, I did point out that I would always answer questions – and *that's* something she has never forgotten. I now affectionately refer to her as my own personal Columbo – 'Just one more thing ...'

I don't always see the need for so many words. My texts are short and to the point: yes, no, ok, no problemo. Hers, on the other hand, spill over into multi-text essays. My phone calls have a purpose and end when it's fulfilled. Hers are long, involving a myriad of asides, and she often forgets why she rang in the first place, making a second call necessary.

If I've got something important to say, I say it once. She says it in three different ways to make sure that someone's really got the picture.

For two people who have so much else in common, our talking habits couldn't be more different. But together we work.

I'd like to say that's because she talks and I listen. But that's not strictly true. I have my own amazing ability to zone out and think about important things when her words start coming closer together and slowly turn into white noise in my head. Sadly, she has a sixth sense and knows when this has happened – incredibly even on the telephone – and generally puts a stop to it pretty fast.

The reason we work is because of the questions. My wife has discovered the way to know me; to know what's going on in my head. She helps me to talk by knowing what I need to talk about or what she needs to hear and prompting me. To be fair it's a two-way thing – bizarrely, when she's upset, my wife loses the ability to communicate. She goes quiet and then it's my turn to goad the information out of her.

But this communication, this talking that I sometimes feel

is so overrated, is vital to our relationship. It's how we learn about each other; it's how we grow closer and how we build the rest of our lives together.

It's the same with our children. We need to take the time to hear about their day – the things that have gone well, the upsets they have had, and the fears that have cast frowns across their faces. We need to take the time to make sure they know that we love them, that we're proud of them and will support them in the things that they do. And we need to make time, not just to discipline them, but to explain why, to challenge them and help them grow, and to encourage them in the people that they are becoming.

In all our relationships, communication is key. It's the same in our relationship with God. It's vital that we take time to talk to God and time to listen to Him – without glazing over and thinking of the football scores. If we are to grow in our relationship with Him, we need to get to know Him – to read the Bible, with all the glimpses into His character that that gives us. And we need to pray – to tell God what is on our hearts, what our worries are, our dreams, and to discover His dreams for us.

Not that God doesn't know what is going on in our lives – the Bible clearly tells us that He does: *'Your Father knows what you need before you ask him'* (Matthew 6:8). No, prayer is about relationship. God just likes to spend time with us.

My wife tells me that the good thing about me being a quiet type is that when I do share a part of myself with her, it feels as though she has been given a treasure. I suspect God feels the same way about all of us.

19

VENTING MY SPLEEN

I don't know if you have watched the programme, *Lead Balloon*. It features a wonderful character called Rick Spleen, played by deadpan comic, Jack Dee. He is a grumpy, frustrated stand-up comedian whose life is full of petty annoyances and let-downs. It's a favourite in our house, possibly because my wife thinks that the writers must have based the character on me.

Don't get me wrong – I am generally an optimistic, the glass is half-full kind of guy. But I have my moments when I quote the great Victor Meldrew and roll my eyes at the situations I find myself in.

I don't think I'm alone. I'm sure most people can empathise with the frustration of having waited in a queue in Iceland for the best part of a lifetime behind a dear old soul who has bought 50 marked down items that all need the label peeling off the bar code to scan, who has someone to pack her bags for her, but who, when the check-out assistant totals the bill, says, 'Oh, now where did I put my purse?' She's had the last ten minutes to dig it out and be ready to pay. Honestly.

The other day I was shopping for a gift for my wife in one of those shops designed to frustrate blokes – full of necklaces, hats, scarves and bizarre little trinkets that serve no purpose I can fathom. Seriously, how many necklaces can one woman have – or wear for that matter? As for hats – don't get me started.

Anyway, the gentleman in front of me in the queue appeared to be buying Christmas presents for every female member in his extended family – and perhaps for all those who lived within a 50-mile radius of his house. When the assistant asked if he would like his purchases gift wrapped, he of course said yes, easily tripling the amount of time I was going to have to wait. And then, when the wrapping, and bows, and stickers were completed, and the admittedly eye-watering total was announced, he had the gobsmacking audacity to say, 'Gosh, that's rather expensive; I don't think I have enough.' You can only imagine how long it took to unwrap each gift, and decide which items he would leave. It took all my willpower not to bang my head against the counter.

And then there are traffic wardens. Sitting in my favourite café the other day, supping a large skinny latte (half the calories but all the taste) I watched as not one, but two traffic wardens walked past a car parked illegally outside. They walked around it and then walked on, even though the owner was causing an obstruction. It wasn't that I wanted the pretty woman who had parked there to get a ticket, it was that I just knew, had it been me, I would have got a ticket. Not because I'm not a pretty lady but because, isn't that just the way?

And I've not even mentioned noisy eaters, people who read out loud what they're typing in an email, roadworks on the M1, bad grammar, fussy eaters, London, people whistling out of tune, opening a DVD case to enjoy a movie and finding the DVD isn't there, BT, children's hand-prints on my plasma telly and those irritating people who say, 'It's always in the last place you look'.

It's not that I vent my frustrations at these people themselves, the streets are safe; I'm not patrolling the towns giving people what for. Instead I tend to go home and express my outrage to my wife who generally listens, pats me on the head and laughs at me. But these things really can stew within me – I tell my wife, then the guys at the gym, and then the children when they get home from school. It can't be good for me.

In fact the Bible says it isn't. Actually, what the Bible has to say is thought provoking – *'Do not be quickly provoked in your spirit, for anger resides in the lap of fools'* (Ecclesiastes 7:11). I prefer not think of myself as a fool. But I have to face it. The irritation that I feel in these situations, the frustration that sets in, achieves nothing but a pain in the side of my head and maybe the wry amusement of my family.

I can't even claim righteous anger; I'm simply getting wound up and, in the words of the great Take That, 'I need a little patience'. Perhaps I could even help the old dear at the checkout who, for all I know, is having the only human contact in her day, or say something to soothe the embarrassment of the gentleman who doesn't have enough money to pay for his kind gifts.

Because what we see as irritations can be transformed into so much more. They can all be opportunities to demonstrate God's love in action; chances to show kindness, patience and self control – gifts of the Spirit which we can share with those around us, helping them to get a glimpse into God's heart for them.

Maybe then, too, my wife would stop calling me Rick.

20

KHATYN

I have just returned from a trip to the beautiful country of Belarus, a former Soviet State in Eastern Europe, located just north of the Ukraine with Russia to the east. I often travel to this part of the world but this time I saw something that will stay with me for a very long time.

It was a cold, crisp January day and snow lay a foot thick on the ground as we visited Khatyn; a ghost town memorial to a village that once was. Here during World War Two, 149 people, including 75 precious children, lost their lives.

The German occupation of Belarus had been long and brutal and, as in the Western countries that we know more about, there were brave resistance movements fighting to liberate their country from the oppressors.

The Nazis' failure to subdue the population caused embarrassment and led to fiercer and fiercer retaliations to assert their dominance and retain their pride. On March 22nd 1943, Belarusian guerrillas fired on a fascist motor convoy on the Minsk – Vitebsk motorway near Khatyn. It consisted of a passenger car and two trucks.

As a result of the strafing attack, a police officer, Hauptmann Welke – the chief commander of the 1st company of the 118th police battalion, and three other policemen were killed. A German Punishment Battalion burnt the village of Khatyn to the ground as a reprisal whilst the inhabitants watched.

They then herded the villagers into a barn and covered the roof with straw. At first the captives had no idea what the Germans intended to do, but as they smelt the kerosene being poured on the building and saw the flames start to lick at the doors, mass panic broke out. In an attempt to save the children they were thrown from the windows where the Germans waited to mow them down with machine gun fire. The youngest baby was only seven weeks old.

Only one man survived – he'd been out of town on a business trip and returned the following day to find his house burned down, his family gone and only the bullet ridden body of his son to show they had ever existed.

These days Khatyn is kept as a national monument to the bravery and sacrifice of Belarus' ancestors. Its memorial stands proud amongst the stone chimneys that survived the fire, bells attached to each one to toll every minute, remembering those burnt alive on that terrible spring day.

Perhaps most poignant of all is the statue of the survivor – the man who never left his village; who stayed there always to tend the graves of his loved ones and to preserve the monument to their memory.

Khatyn was not the only village to be treated in such a way. Belarus suffered terribly during the war. Among the best-recognized symbols is a monument with three birch trees, and an eternal flame instead of a fourth tree, a tribute to the one in every four Belarusians who died in the war. There is also a statue of Yuzif Kaminsky carrying his dying son.

The site also contains a wall with niches to represent the victims of all concentration camps, the large niches standing for concentration camps with victims of greater than 20,000 people. Teddy bears have been left by visitors in some, to remember the children. Thousands were sent to child concentration camps where, fed only on water, their blood was used for transfusions to save the lives of wounded German officers. Children rarely survived more than a month.

Belarus was part of the land called Lebensraum or 'living space' by Hitler. He believed that Germany needed more room, and he looked to the East to find it. Here lived a people that he held to be inferior to his Aryan race – an expendable people who stood in his way. In his world order, Social Darwinism meant the fittest would survive, so decimating the population of an inferior nation was just natural.

It was a day out that I will never forget. Stories like this stagger the mind and sicken the soul. What one man can do to another is beyond our grasp. And all because one man thought he was better than another.

We may not be plotting genocide or the take over of

another country, but it got me thinking – how often have we felt a little superior to those around us? To the girls behind the checkout in Tesco, or the guys working in MacDonald's? How many times have we secretly thanked God that we weren't born on that estate or into that family? When have we thought that someone didn't deserve to win the lottery and wouldn't they just waste all that money? And when have we looked down on those from a different culture or religion?

It is very easy to start feeling a little proud of our standing, our intelligence, our wealth or our family. Maybe even of our race or our gender. The reality is that God made us all equal. My wife is a maths teacher and is quick to point out that equal does not mean that two things are the same but that they have the same value. It's a lesson we need to apply to more than just algebra. Each of us is precious to God in our unique and wonderful ways. If we are to become more like Him then we must start to value our neighbours as He does.

21

INDECENT EXPOSURE

The comedians, Cannon and Ball, were my childhood comedy heroes. Every Saturday evening would see me sitting down in front of the TV to watch Bobby winding Tommy up. Because of this, I was thrilled when in 1986 I heard that Bobby had become a Christian – as a young Christian myself I was really encouraged by this and started praying regularly for Tommy. Six years later he, too, became a Christian and the two decided to use their talents to share the Gospel.

I was over the moon to be invited to be part of their Gospel Tour, in theatres and arenas all around the country. We performed to more than 50,000 people over 48 nights during 1995. It was the stuff of my dreams – performing with my favourite comedians, becoming their friend and sharing Jesus with people all at once. It was a busy and exciting time with more than the planned laughs.

We travelled the length and breadth of the country and it

was a wonderful experience. Bob and Tom were the stars of the show, but the cast also featured solo singer, Danny Owen, and duo, Perfect Match, all backed by a five-piece band, as well as yours truly.

Each night, I'd open the second half, appearing out of an empty box, to be manacled into a regulation strait jacket from which I attempted to extricate myself faster than Houdini, but with a daring difference. I escaped upside-down whilst dangling from the top of the theatre. All went well until a show at Edinburgh's magnificent King's Theatre.

The kindly organisers took us out for a slap-up, all-inclusive, eat as much as you possibly can, Chinese buffet meal before the show. Just two hours later, our crew waited in the wings armed with buckets as I dangled upside down, turning various shades of green, escaping from the strait jacket, whilst trying not to be violently sick all over the stage. Forget escapology – keeping my dinner down was the most impressive thing I did all day.

Some years later, we were back together again for a big outdoor event in Sefton Park, Liverpool, where we had a very unfortunate incident involving one of those clever one-way mirrors – you can see out but people can't see in. It was to be one of the most embarrassing moments of my life – and believe me, I've had a few.

The show itself was a huge affair organised by local churches and we had an awesome roadshow vehicle for the day – a bit like those used for the Radio One Roadshow – a stage out front and changing rooms and a lounge area at the side. It made you feel like a real star.

Hanging out backstage, Bobby and I enjoyed a cup of coffee in the lounge, having a laugh and reminiscing, when we realised we were on next and needed to get changed. We stared out of the lounge windows at the crowds.

'These one-way mirrors are amazing, aren't they?' I said to Bobby as we started getting undressed. He agreed and we both stopped what we were doing and stared at the crowd, wondering how many people were out there.

I'm not sure how long we stood there in our underpants before we spotted some women giggling. We didn't have time to wonder why – shortly after, their pointing fingers made it perfectly clear as they mouthed the words, 'Look, it's Bobby Ball.' They probably didn't mouth it; they probably said it loudly. It's just that we were watching all this through what was clearly *not* special one-way glass. The very normal glass was all that stood between our pants and the vast crowd who had come to hear us tell them about Jesus.

Frozen to the spot, we realised we had been entertaining the crowds in a quite unplanned and most unexpected way. I belatedly caught sight of the curtains at the side of the window and swiftly pulled them. It was one of those moments that stick in your mind; two decent, God-fearing men standing with their hands on their hips in their underpants in front of an enormous crowd of people waiting to hear them talk about God. We had been caught very much, with our pants up.

It's easy to get a feeling of security when we're Christians, to think that somehow we're untouchable, that no one can see what we're doing. We can get carried away with our positions in life, forgetting that the glass is just glass and we're not protected by a magic mirror that gives us a great view but let's no one else get a look in. Bobby and I got caught strutting our stuff in a 'man in the locker room' type of way, but there have been too many falls from grace by men and women who thought their positions protected them.

It is at our peril that we think we are beyond the watching eyes of the world when we do things we know we shouldn't, and it is pure foolishness to think that God doesn't know our thoughts let alone see our actions. We are called to be His light in this world, to shine like stars in the universe, so let's concentrate on doing exactly that.

In Matthew's Gospel, Jesus told us not to hide our light under a bucket. Let's not put anything under a bucket. In fact, let's throw away the bucket and live our lives in the open for everyone to see, and make sure that we live lives to bring honour to Jesus.

One more point. It has angered and really saddened me to see how we treat those whose indiscretions have been revealed. It is amazing how fast someone can go from being everyone's best friend to a complete pariah. People who have stood and shared the limelight start denying their former hero and distancing themselves. We should never condone wrongdoing, but equally we should never abandon our friends. God never writes people off, and neither should we.

22

BY THE BOOK

My dad is a draftsman, my brother is a draftsman. Order and precision are in my genes. True, I have followed a somewhat different career path – no hanging upside down from a crane whilst wriggling out of a regulation straitjacket for the other men in my family (to be fair there probably isn't room for more than one escapologist in any family), but that sense of fine detail and organisation runs deep inside my veins.

When I was a single dad with four kids, I ran my house like a military operation. For five years we had routines that ran like clockwork. Everything had its place in the house and everyone knew where that was. Then I met my new wife. Her routines were not my own – in fact, routine is a word that brings her out in hives. My world has changed.

Years ago I heard cookery queen, Delia Smith, mention that once toast has popped up, it should be left for a minute before you take it out of the toaster and butter it. Something to do with the time gap allowing the molecules to slow down apparently, so the toast won't be soggy. So that's why I leave my toast for precisely (and I do mean precisely) 60 seconds before applying butter and marmalade. For some reason I can't quite fathom, my wife thinks it's a little strange and complains about cold toast.

That's just the start. I don't think I'm that unusual, but it's the little things I like – all my DVDs stored in alphabetical order, for example. Then there's the cutlery drawer. I like the knives and forks lined up and nestled in each other – tidy and ordered. The first time my wife emptied the dishwasher she threw the teaspoons into the drawer in a jumbled up fashion, all in the teaspoon compartment admittedly, but facing in different directions like a metallic nest for a bird with no thought to comfort or order.

I bit my tongue and quietly tidied them up when she wasn't looking. I then opened the crockery cupboard to see that she had piled the kids' plastic plates on top of the ceramic ones. Call me pedantic, but I prefer to keep my plastics and ceramics safely apart – it's not an obsession, of course, but I really can't settle knowing they are together.

Again though, I quietly put the four plastic plates back in the plastic plate cupboard, until I went to get a glass of water and discovered to my horror that she had put the glasses back in the cupboard the wrong way up and out of line. It was time for some staff training.

Bewildered, Rebekah wondered aloud how severe my OCD was. What was the point she asked, of having an entire cupboard devoted to four plastic plates just because they were made of a different material to the others? I struggled to explain that when you allow plastic and ceramic plates to mix in the same place it's the start of a slippery slope to chaos and anarchy. She thought I was joking.

I managed to convince her that storing glasses upside-down stops them collecting bugs and dirt, though I did compromise on the ordered lines of glasses that I prefer queued up like a military parade. In turn Rebekah has learnt to nestle the teaspoons together in a way that lets me sleep soundly at night.

Household orderliness aside, I am also a stickler for punctuality. I am routinely early. I take no prisoners when it comes to leaving the house on time; I don't answer the phone if it rings on my way out of the door and I don't stop to chat if I'm on the way to a meeting.

I have to get the children to school for 8:50am but I prefer to be there by 8:30am as this enables me to get parked next to the school gate. The gates don't actually open till 8:40am but we have time to relax, listen to the news on the radio and watch the taxi driver arrive with a steaming hot coffee for the lollipop lady. We then know it is time to get out of the car and wait for another ten minutes in the playground. Rain or shine this is what we do.

Or rather did. Rebekah has a more tenuous grasp of the school routine. She considers the ten minutes in the car a waste of time, let alone the ten minutes shivering in the playground. She always tries to cram one more job in before she leaves the house and is totally incapable of ignoring the telephone. I can get a little tense and have to confess to counting the seconds down audibly in case she hasn't realised that she is running out of time. But to be fair she has never got the children to school late. She just does things differently to me.

I love my wife dearly and I'd have changed the world for her – maybe even have let go of the teaspoon chaos. But accepting people's quirks and understanding their differences can be a difficult thing, and nowhere does this seem to be more pronounced than in the church. We build up our routines and traditions, we get set in our ways and when change comes we get uncomfortable, we get stubborn and sometimes, if we're honest, we get unkind.

Jesus shook up people's lives; He didn't always do things in the accepted way. He challenged people's beliefs and questioned their long held traditions. There's no point in being radical for radical's sake, but let's not get so caught up in doing things our way that we can't let the unusual in and do things a little differently.

And let's never let the differences get in the way of our relationships. Holding on to our traditions and resisting change at the expense of our friendships is foolish to the point of stupidity. If I'd have held on to the plastic/ceramic divide and Rebekah had continued to rebel, we could have lost the happiness we have now.

It's a daft example I know, but how many times do we prioritise our routines over other people's feelings? We need to learn to compromise, to talk things through, to spend time understanding someone else's point of view and sometimes we need to make room for a little change.

After all, the world probably won't end if a teaspoon points south for one night.

23

PLANE CRAZY

I have a bit of an eye for a bargain. I always like to think I'm getting a good deal on my purchases, whether that is a new car, a loft conversion or, if I'm perfectly honest, a packet of custard creams.

My family despair of me; they have no appreciation of the fine art of the barter. They don't seem impressed when I ask the woman behind the till in Tesco if she can cut me a deal if I buy my pasta in bulk. They don't understand that if you save the pennies the pounds look after themselves and that if you don't ask you don't get.

My wife refers to me as Del Boy and my children stand on the other side of the shop so as not to be associated with me; but I am undeterred. I could haggle for England, save a penny and feel as though my day was full of sunshine for the saving.

So it was that on a cold autumn afternoon a couple of weeks ago, I checked in for my flight with a couple of friends at Belfast

Airport. As we were about to go through security and into the departure lounge, a sign caught my eye: 'Free refills when you buy a large coffee'. Well, that was it. Why go through to the departure lounge when such a caffeine bargain was to be had this side of the security gate?

And bargain it was – never have I enjoyed a skinny latte so much, and the pleasure only increased as I moved on to my free refill. By the time I was on my third cup, my happiness had reached a level only matched by the caffeine buzzing around my system and the intense pressure on my bladder. I was in free coffee heaven.

Adrian and I had been sharing funny airport stories when my other pal and fellow traveller, Mark, raised the query that perhaps we should head through security so as to be ready when they called our flight. But I had my eye on one last refill, and confidently assured him that security never takes more than five minutes in Belfast. I savoured my last mug, made a vital visit to the gents and then set off to the departure lounge.

Forty minutes later I was still standing in the queue, shoes in my hand, being patted down by a surly Irish security guard and having to explain why I had an egg whisk (one of my daft props) in my hand baggage. Legs crossed, desperate to relieve myself of the third and fourth refills, I groaned as I heard the announcement that our gate was now closing. We had missed the flight. My free coffee cost me £70 in new tickets.

The situation raised some chuckles at home but it did make me think – rarely do you get something for nothing. I'm not taking it away from Starbucks, they weren't out to fleece me – they really did intend for me to have free refills. It was my lack of judgement that made me miss the plane. But it took my mind to that other free gift that I have. The gift of life itself.

God offers us the most amazing life. He offers us freedom from the mistakes that we've made and, like the coffee, we can just keep going back for more. There is no end to the forgiveness, the special offer doesn't have a time frame – God's love just keeps on coming. The best bit of all is that there are no hidden clauses, no sly agendas. I'm not going to get caught at God's gate looking for the cash to pay for a new ticket.

The price of my freedom has already been paid in full.

24

PUTTING MY FOOT IN IT

When it comes to sleep, I'm a man who knows what he likes. I like to sleep in the dark. Proper dark – none of this, leaving a light on for the kids, nonsense. I don't like the street lights shining through the curtains or the LED from the mobile phone boring small red holes in my psyche. I'd be happiest going to sleep in the desert with the stars turned out.

I like quiet, too. No music playing in the background, no children padding round the house. No wife trying to engage me in conversation in the wee hours.

And when I'm tired I like to go to sleep immediately. So I turn out the lights and roll over; even though my wife is still cleaning her teeth in the bathroom. The frustrating thing is her inability to come to bed quietly – she generally turns out the bathroom light quietly enough, but then complains about the dark, not taking the hint at all that night time is upon us and I am trying to sleep. She proceeds to stumble around kicking various pieces of furniture loudly – yelping each time. She has even gone so far as to turn the light back on, with no warning whatsoever, to find her pyjamas.

I just don't get it – what requires so much noise? And why on earth would you turn the lights back on when someone has turned them off? Clearly I have signed out for the night and should not be disturbed. I don't see what the problem is – there is even some light that still comes in through the window, so the dramatic kicking of furniture is incomprehensible and, as for more light – totally unnecessary.

I really didn't understand what my wife's problem was. But one night, she apparently thought that I was huffing and puffing melodramatically about the noise she was making, and instead of letting me huff under the duvet away from the light, made me get out of bed, totally disturbing my drift off to Neverland.

She then marched me to the bathroom, turned on the light and made me stay there for two minutes before switching the light off and pushing me out into the dark, instructing me to head for bed. 'No problemo,' I announced. I then proceeded to collide with three pieces of furniture before tripping over the end of the bed.

It took my wife five minutes to stop laughing. And I got the point.

There's an old Indian saying that you should walk a mile in another man's moccasins before judging, but for me it just took the length of our bedroom in my wife's darkness. I didn't even need to put her pink slippers on. Instead of just moaning at her inability to navigate the bedroom in the darkness, I finally realised what it was like for her to try and do that, and now I have changed how I behave. I leave the light on.

A different man may not have needed the lesson, and I'm aware that there are women everywhere outraged that I ever turned the light off in the first place. But there are times for all of us when we judge a situation without ever really understanding it. We judge people's reactions to things without stopping to think what it must be like for them. We need to put ourselves in the shoes of those around us a little more often.

It's what God did. He didn't sit in heaven huffing and puffing about a world that turned its back on Him. He didn't roll His eyes and wonder what our problem was. God never lay down, pulling the duvet over His eyes while His loved ones stumbled and fell.

Instead He came and lived as one of us. Not for two minutes but for 33 long years. Hard years – years of poverty, years when no one understood who He was, not even His parents; years when He struggled with who He was and what He had to do; years when He felt alone and afraid, and years that ended with Him dying someone else's death. God, in His Son, Jesus, lived through everything we could ever face. He understands fully what it is to be us, because He has been there.

It is a most wonderful thing to know that our God, Creator of the universe, Lord of heaven and earth has truly walked in our pink slippers.

25

MY LITTLE MIRACLE

Babies are frightening things. When they are first born, they are even more so – tiny, fragile and helpless. I distinctly remember when Amber, my first daughter, was born – worrying that I would break her if I picked her up, wanting to wrap her in cotton wool to keep her safe. I had been given this precious and most wonderful gift and I would have given my life to protect her – I still would.

Everything was new to me. I learned to master the nappies, warm the bottle and test the temperature of the bath. I learned the best way to hold her when she cried for no apparent reason, and discovered that stroking her face calmed her down. I was learning all the time but little things could make me worry that something was wrong – when she wouldn't sleep I worried something was the matter, and when she stayed asleep for too long, I worried again. But I put my baby in God's care and trusted that He would look after her.

My faith in this was really put to the test just seven weeks after Amber was born. Overnight she became very ill – she couldn't keep her milk down and she was crying endlessly – the kind of crying that really does mean something is wrong. She was swiftly taken into hospital for tests.

Amber was so tiny and had become so dehydrated that it took the doctors hours to get a drip into her little arm. She had endless blood tests and a lumbar puncture to try and assess what the matter was. Eventually an x-ray revealed the problem – the lower part of her bowel was twisted. It was a dangerous condition that needed immediate attention.

We were quickly transferred by ambulance to Brighton's fantastic children's hospital, where the operation to restore Amber's gut could be performed. I went with Amber and the nurses as she was taken for more x-rays in preparation for the operation. I watched, helpless, as doctors pushed tubes into my baby's nose and down into her little stomach to give her barium to help them see the extent of the problem.

And I watched, amazed, as the radiographers started shaking their heads and called the consultant to say that they didn't understand it, but the problem seemed to have rectified itself. They took three different x-rays to be sure but finally turned to tell me that there was no need for an operation. They couldn't explain it, but there was no longer anything wrong with my daughter.

Overjoyed, I told them that I could explain. As soon as Amber had become ill, we had phoned friends from church and ever since then people had been praying for her. I explained that I believed in a God who can and does perform miracles and that today we had all seen Him do just that. The doctor just kept shaking his said and saying that he didn't understand it.

I've often thought, how amazing to have been alive when Jesus walked the earth – to see Him help lame people get to their feet, to watch Him give sight to the blind. Just imagine walking with Him on water. I can't help thinking that it would be easier to believe if you could just see something spectacular. But the truth is, even when people do witness a miracle, they don't always *see* it. Jesus' own disciples doubted Him; men who had watched Him heal people right in front of them, shouted for Him to be crucified.

I love the clip in the movie, *Bruce Almighty*, where Morgan Freeman, cast as God, tells Bruce that 'parting' his tomato soup was a magic trick, not a miracle – he goes on to say that miracles are 'a single mum who holds down two jobs and still finds time to take her child to soccer practice. A miracle is a kid who says "no" to drugs and "yes" to an education'.

We see God working around us all the time – sometimes in dramatic ways and sometimes in small ways; sometimes He whispers to us through the dawn of a new day and other times He shouts His love to us through the sheer beauty of His creation. We can become deaf to His voice and blind to His works and because of that, we miss out on all that He can give us.

Let's not block God out of our lives. Instead let's give God the credit for the work He never stops doing. Let's listen to the overtures of love that He has for us and let's revel in the miracles that we find all around us.

I, for one, will never stop thanking God for my little miracle.

26

PANIC AT THE PUMPS

I like to get to gigs on time. I don't do last minute rushes. I leave with plenty of time to spare and some more besides. I have my routine. I get my gear together the night before and have it ready to pack in the car. In the morning I get up, shower, shave, do my hair, get dressed and eat my breakfast. The OCD does not dictate what I eat, so this can vary.

Then, I pack my car, drive to the BP station on the junction with the dual carriageway, and fill the tank with diesel. I always choose BP to keep the continuity with the Nectar points. I then drive to wherever I'm going, usually arrive with at least an hour to spare and sit quietly and read the paper. It's what I do and it works.

It's what I tried to do one Saturday afternoon last year. I had successfully completed most of my routine. I was showered and shaved; I'd cleaned my teeth and my hair was perfection. I had packed my car and double-checked that I had everything. My suit was hanging up so it wouldn't crease. All that remained was to get the fuel. This function, too, was performed like clockwork.

Our local petrol station is one of those with a mini supermarket attached. Less of a supermarket and more of a well-named corner shop really, but nonetheless very useful if you want to pick up a pint of milk on your way home. Not very useful when the person who is parked at the pump in front of you is doing their weekly shop for a family of ten. This is what happened the day that I had completed all but the last part of my routine.

I was all paid up, had got back in my car and was just waiting for the guy in front of me to finish and pay. He put the petrol cap back on, locked his door and went in. He then proceeded to pick up a basket and start shopping. Initially I wasn't perturbed – a pint of milk wouldn't throw the schedule. After a few minutes, I glanced at my watch – this was taking longer than I had imagined. I went to reverse out of the station, but as I put the car in gear, a large 4x4 pulled in behind me. There was no way out. I began to get nervous. My routine was being threatened – pushed out of kilter, and that makes me uncomfortable.

I thought perhaps it was like a watched pot never boiling, so I studiously looked in the opposite direction, willing the man to be back in his car when I turned round. Instead he had just moved to the chilled aisle. This was getting ridiculous. I tried not to watch him as he moved slowly around the shop, but my eyes became fixated as he ambled about. He even picked up a second basket. I was beside myself.

Eventually after what seemed like hours – but was probably just ten minutes – he finished. He paid for his goods and lumbered out with all his shopping bags. He then proceeded to load his groceries into the boot, hunting around in one of the bags to find a Twix which he slowly unwrapped before nodding cheerily at me and getting into his car. I started my engine in preparation, wiping the beads of sweat from my fevered brow.

There was no need. Doctor Dawdle was rummaging around in his car looking for something else – his hat. He found it, put it on, adjusted it in the mirror and then re-adjusted the mirror. Next came his brown, leather driving gloves. Finally, *finally* he started the engine – before turning it off, getting back out of the car and returning to the shop. He'd forgotten to buy cigarettes. It was as close as I have come to spontaneous combustion.

Eventually, of course, he moved the car and I got on my way – although I didn't arrive in time to read more than the sports section of the paper. For a while there, however, I wondered if I was just going to wait in the car all day – all ready to go but not actually going anywhere. I wonder how often we do that?

We get all prepared to do something but find an obstacle in our way. All kinds of things – maybe we had an idea for an event we could put on at our church but some bureaucratic nonsense stood in our way; or we decided to visit someone who needed a friend, but our diary just seemed so busy. It might have been as simple as choosing to go to house group but at the end of the day we were just too tired.

Maybe we've heard all there is to know about God. We know who He is; we know what we have to do. But something is stopping us from making the decision and asking Him to walk with us through life. Anything can become an obstacle if we let it.

The thing is, in hindsight, drumming my fingers on the steering wheel didn't really help the situation. Neither did staring in the opposite direction. What might have had an effect was if I had got out of my seat, strolled across the forecourt and into the shop and actually asked the gentleman if he would mind moving his car. It's not rocket science. But it's not quite British either – I felt far less awkward sitting and stewing than getting up and asking a man I didn't know to interrupt his shopping.

As God's people we have been blessed with His gifts. We are His hands, His feet and His heart. We mustn't let things get in the way of completing His mission. Obstacles will come and difficulties will occur, make no mistake, but we have a God who can move mountains so let's work with Him to push those obstacles aside. Let's stand together, take hold of our gifts and follow our leader into the adventure of our lives.

And if you're waiting in the forecourt, putting off the decision to follow God, it's time to get out of your seat and start walking.

27

JUST DO IT

I've heard it said that children are sent to try us. That may be true. What is most definitely true is that they are sent to embarrass us. Megan, my youngest, is one of the most literal beings on earth and whatever is on her mind comes straight out of her mouth. Whereas some of the other children need coaxing to tell you what's going on in their lives, Meg just lets it all out – I'm tired, I'm angry, your breath is stinky, I feel like dancing; you get the idea. There is no sacred territory with her.

This is why it is wise to watch what you say around her. You'd think I might have learned that simple lesson by now. I love to tease the kids and nothing winds them up more than getting their teachers' names muddled up. Headteacher, the wonderful Mr White, becomes Mr Purple; I call Mr Elwood by his Christian name and Gemma goes berserk because, 'Dad! He's not called Stevie E., he's called Mr Elwood'. She's horrified at the thought that I may call him by his first name in public and shame her.

Not Megan. She goes into class and the first thing she says to the lovely Mrs Illsley, the teaching assistant in Year One, is – 'My dad calls you Mrs White Hair because you have white hair like my granny'. I now collect my children in shades and a baseball cap.

My disguise is going to have to get more elaborate. Just this afternoon, I was watching my ten-year-old, Emmie, play netball after school. My other girls were watching with me, when they weren't running around the playground playing 'stuck in the mud'. Megan came running up when she wasn't 'stuck', grabbed my hand and pulled it until I looked at her, and then informed me that she was so desperate she could wet herself.

Keen not to have to stage a mopping-up operation in the playground, I suggested that she should ask Mrs Flint, our faithful, friendly and ever so helpful receptionist, if she could let her into school to use the toilet. She promptly followed my suggestion, and the crisis was averted.

Meanwhile, back on the netball pitch – if that's what you call it – all was well. Emmie defended some brave attempts on goal and the half time whistle went. Out came the orange quarters just like I remembered from football matches when I was at school.

'That brings back memories,' I reminisced out loud. 'Megan, go and see if they've got a spare orange for me,' I *joked*.

Distracted by a message on my BlackBerry, I didn't see her march over to the makeshift table to ask the netball mums if her dad could have some orange.

It was hard to know where to look when she came back

with an orange quarter for me amidst some strange looks from the netball mums. I attempted to usher her away and explain that I didn't really want it; I even tried to convince *her* to eat it because I thought it would look better for me, if worse for her. But she wasn't having any of it – 'But, Dad, you said … !' I ate it before she protested any more loudly and just kept my eyes away from the disapproving mums.

With hindsight, I'm not really sure why, five minutes later, I mentioned that I, too, was desperate, having been seduced into two large lattes in the coffee shop an hour earlier. I certainly have no idea why I joked to Meg that perhaps she should ask Mrs Flint if I, too, could use the school toilets.

Meg's sense of humour really doesn't run along the same lines as mine. It's barely in the same universe. Sure enough, when I was concentrating on telling Emmie to tickle her opponent when she was trying to shoot – apparently an illegal move in netball – and consequently being glowered at again by the netball mums, Megan disappeared.

The next I knew of it was when Mrs Flint literally dashed out of the door shouting, 'Mr Legg, of course you can use our loo if you're desperate!'

I needed to go home. Fast.

The other girls laughed and teased Meggie who got a bit upset because she couldn't understand what she'd done wrong. I had to step in and point out that actually Megan had been fantastic. She'd done exactly what she had been asked and she'd got the job sorted. She'll make a fine businesswoman one day – getting the netball mums to hand over an orange – what a feat.

I think sometimes we could all learn a lesson from Megan. She didn't question her father, she just obeyed him.

So often in our Christian lives we're more of a Jonah, second guessing God and trying to mould His will to ours. That childlike obedience is something to strive for – to walk into situations that are daunting because our Father has asked us to.

Jonah heard God calling him to talk to his enemies and he ran in the opposite direction and ended up stuck inside a gigantic fish. He couldn't believe God really meant what He said, so he did the opposite. He thought he knew better and tried to impose his own ideas on God's plan for the world.

We all do it – try to persuade God that He's really calling us to ministry in the Bahamas with a pool and a Porsche. Maybe not quite that, but we hope He's calling us to stay within our comfort zones and minister to those we love already.

It can go against the grain to be friendly to the guy at work who makes David Brent look like Captain Cool. It hurts sometimes to take the time to say 'hi' to the woman in the playground who we know has spread nasty stories about us. Sometimes it's sheer hard work to get motivated after a long day, and help out at the youth club. But if it's what God's asking us to do, we need to do it.

Let's listen out for God's plan for our lives with an open heart and a willing mind. Let's not try and second guess what He has in store for us. Instead let's have that simple, childlike obedience and walk with faith into the amazing adventure God has lined up for us.

And always, always watch what you say to small children.

28

ROAD TO NOWHERE

Skiing or sunbathing? There's a choice – actually, for me there's no competition; I'd go for a summer holiday every time. My wife loves skiing but when she goes she leaves me behind – I simply do not get the appeal of standing at the top of a perilous incline in the bitter cold before hurling yourself down a mountain on a pair of planks waving a couple of sharp sticks around as you go.

No, I'm a true English gentleman who sits out in the midday sun lapping up the warmth as it slowly roasts me. I love the heat – I get into a steaming bath and then keep running the hot tap until I resemble a lobster. I love a sauna, too, and have been known to spend more time sweating in the Swedish wooden box at the gym than working out on the cross trainer.

But there are limits, and the 17 hours that I spent in a sauna thinly disguised as a Ukrainian train went way beyond them. Two days earlier I had flown with a group into Simferapol, a town in the south of the country lying on the Salgir River where it emerges from the Crimean Mountains, just minutes from Yalta – that historical city that few of us can place on a map.

I'd been performing for some of the poorest children in the country in hospitals, orphanages and street shelters, and was en route to the capital, Kiev, in the north, to entertain more little ones. Alan, our group organiser (who interestingly didn't accompany us on the tortuous train trip) had decided we should travel by train – for the cultural experience.

I have had better cultural experiences in the bargain aisle in Tesco. The train was less Orient Express and more shabby wooden crate on wheels. In each crate are tiny compartments called *kupes* in which four people are jammed like sardines. When you need to relieve yourself you have to run the gauntlet of the corridor, stepping over bags and avoiding the frighteningly named *provodnitsa* attending each carriage, to get to the dirty hole in the floor which passes for a toilet. I'm not even going to try to describe the fears that pass through your mind as you attempt to hover and aim with a cold blast of air shooting straight up through the opening, whilst watching the train tracks rattle past below you.

Crammed into a tiny *kupe* with three people I barely knew – one of whom, a dour Scotsman called Alistair, stripped down to his blue underpants within minutes of entering the cabin – I spent the first few hours working out how to fold my 6' 3" frame into the 5' 2" bunk bed. Having miraculously accomplished this feat, I started to become aware of the incredible heat that seemed to come out of the very furniture. I folded myself back out of my bed to find the window and took deep breaths of fresh air as I lowered it.

Refreshed, I raised the window again, leaving it open a fraction to let the cold air outside battle the heat within. Professional contortionist that I am, I squeezed back into the foetal position in my bunk and had just closed my eyes when a burly woman (at least I think she was a woman, but I wouldn't stake my life on it) slammed the door open, barked, 'Niet,' and rammed the window closed.

She (he) and her fellow *provodnitsa* were huddled around the source of the heat at the end of the carriage – a wood burning stove surely designed to stoke the fires of hell. I still can't understand how they could sit so close to it without melting unless perhaps their names were Shadrach, Meshach and Abednego. Every time I tried to let in some fresh air they would instantly know and come and seal the heat back in.

This went on for 17 hours as we dawdled across the Ukraine. I lost half my body weight in sweat and consoled myself with the thought that we must be nearly there. Four hours after the train left the station, I braved the window police and stuck my head out to see if I could see how our journey had progressed. I am not exaggerating in the slightest – I could still see the station from which we had departed.

My cultural experience consisted of me learning the frustration of Eastern European travel whilst the words from Talking Heads' 'Road to Nowhere' drifted around my head, and I tried not to dwell on the knowledge that a plane flight for the same journey would have cost less than £30 and we could have been there within the hour.

I had gone through the motions of an epic journey but in reality had only travelled a few hundred yards. Sometimes my life feels a little like that – sweating and stressing but not really achieving anything. We can waste so much time fussing about the little things in life that the important things seem to go by the way.

It's easy to do and something I have had to learn to combat. Each week I spend time with God deciding what I need to achieve by the end of it, and then each day I break those goals down into daily tasks. I have to consciously block out the distractions, not waste my time on things that aren't important.

It's biblical wisdom – Proverbs 4 says, *'Let your eyes look straight ahead, fix your gaze directly before you.'* The writer of Hebrews reaffirms this by declaring, *'Throw off anything that hinders … and run with perseverance the race marked out for us.'*

Let's make goals in all areas of our lives – as parents, as children, as spouses, as friends, and as leaders, as well as in the work place, and let's pursue them wholeheartedly – not letting anything slow us down.

29

TO HULL AND BACK

Since starting out in full-time Christian work, over 20 years ago, I have always loved going into schools to talk about my faith. The challenge of standing up in front of 1400 moody teenagers in assembly on a cold Monday morning and making them laugh, and more importantly making them think about what really matters in life, is a wonderful opportunity and an amazing privilege.

I used to do hundreds of assemblies, as well as a number of special schools' weeks. A band and I would take RE and music lessons, with lunchtime and evening events, too. I travelled far and wide doing dozens of these special missions each year.

One beautiful autumn morning, I headed 'oop North' to Hull, in my pride and joy – my brand new Calypso Capri – for a week of Christian activities in a large secondary school in town. I'd only had the car a week and this was to be the longest outing we had taken together. I remember sitting in the driver's seat, cruising up the M1, gazing out of the windscreen and admiring the enormous power bulge in the middle of the bonnet.

Not that my 1.6 LS version had much oomph really – just 88 brake horsepower would have cantered from the engine when brand spanking new. By the time the '*Silver Bullet*' arrived in my hands, it had frankly seen better days. But on the road it was still a lively thing – not least because of its complete lack of road holding in the wet. It could get to 60mph in about 12.5 seconds, which wasn't bad for a big car with a small engine.

Shallow as I am, what hooked me was the looks – horsepower, torque and thrust aren't words that bother me much – but this car was seriously sexy. My beloved Capri was a limited edition – a striking combination of a two-tone paint scheme – strato silver with graphite grey. It was just like the car Terry McCann drove in ITV's hit comedy-drama *Minder* and I thought I was the bee's knees as I cruised round Littlehampton, windows down, Rayban Aviators on, jacket sleeves rolled up, blaring out my Frankie Goes to Hollywood tape.

The interior was black with red trim and the deeply contoured seats were 100% genuine vinyl. The cockpit felt as if it had been fashioned around me and there was nothing on the road that came close to it. Most would say it had shades of Del Boy in its eighties' excess styling, but I loved the square, aggressive front and long bonnet, and adored the long, sloping tailgate, with curved rear side windows.

As for that black rubber boot spoiler, it might look naff now but back then it looked cool, as if it was there only to keep the back of the car nailed to the road.

Anyway, before I grow a couple of inches, don a brown corduroy jacket and turn into Jeremy Clarkson, I should get back to Hull, where I spent a fantastic week in a secondary school, dealing with the issues that teenagers face and the questions they have. The last day saw me talking about the problem of pain and suffering and why God allows it. It was the end of a great week and, wanting to make a quick and low-key getaway, I packed up, loaded my car, stopped to admire it one more time in the visitors' car park, got in and turned the key in the ignition.

The engine started. I leant over, cranked up the radio and started singing along to 'Loco in Acapulco', stopping mid-sentence as I noticed smoke coming from under the bonnet and then, as I looked closer, realised that the paint was blistering in the centre.

I sat staring at the bubbles for a moment, transfixed by the eruptions. I was jolted out of my reverie by a dinner lady tapping on the window and stating the obvious – my car was on fire. The severity of the situation started to register in my consciousness and I opened the door and leapt out before it blew up. For a few seconds it felt as though I was in a scene from *Miami Vice*.

The dinner lady had dialled 999 and the fire brigade were racing to the scene. Alarms were sounding and moments later, over 1000 children started pouring out of the main doors to the school, evacuated because of the imminent danger. So much for my quiet farewell.

The whole episode was a pretty dramatic way of saying goodbye to the fine people of Hull. For me, the excitement was dissipated somewhat by a 12-hour epic trip home, on no less than three different AA tow trucks, and the fact that my precious car was now a burnt-out shell.

The long journey south gave me plenty of time to grieve the passing of the *Silver Bullet*. And grieve I did. Old and tired as it clearly was, my Capri was my baby and I felt pretty upset that it was gone. I'd saved and scrimped to get it; now I'd not only lost my mode of transport, I'd lost a fair portion of my cool, too. I'd even singed my Don Johnson jacket and it took weeks to get the smell of smoke out of my espadrilles.

I was pretty sorry for myself, and bemoaned the loss of my *precious* to anyone who asked how my week had gone. Which was a shame because the reality is that the week went really well – hundreds of kids got to hear about Jesus and many of them had shown a real interest. The week had been a resounding success.

I'd let myself get too caught up in my possessions. I'd let the car, in a week, get too important to me. It's easy to do. We can treasure our worldly goods so much that we get things out of proportion. We keep our houses so pristine we don't want to let people in. We polish our cars until they shine and are then afraid to use them in case they get scratched. We buy ourselves books, CDs and DVDs, but don't want to share them in case we lose a vital part of our collection.

Looking after our possessions is good stewardship, don't get me wrong, but if we're inhospitable, if we can't give a lift to someone who lives in a rough area, if we can't loan a film to a friend – then something has gone awry. The Bible tells us that these things are temporary – that we shouldn't build storehouses on earth but in heaven. We can always replace the DVD, touch up the car and tidy the house – and, actually, even if it turns out that our friends lose the last ever copy of our favourite film – we can get through the pain and survive. Worse things really do happen to people at sea and considerably closer to home.

Let's not allow our things to become more important than our mission, and let's not judge our success by our possessions. Instead, let's concentrate on fulfilling God's plan in our lives and valuing ourselves as He does.

And let's face it – I don't need a car to be cool – I manage that all by myself.

30

A DATE WITH DEATH

I've said before that I love my job; it has taken me all over the world and into some crazy situations. But it hasn't always been easy. As a young man, I knew that I wanted to spread the Good News on the streets and in schools, but I was a painfully shy person who was afraid of getting things wrong and looking like a doughnut.

It turns out I've looked daft on more than one occasion and in front of more people than I care to count, so my fears were well founded. But I've learnt to face those fears, push through them and do it anyway.

One particularly memorable occasion was in Mexico City back in 1998. I was out there with a small team over the Hallowe'en period, and we found ourselves caught up in the spectacle that is the Day of the Dead. The history behind it is fascinating – native people in Mexico traditionally marked the day by building altars and shrines to ancestors in their homes.

They left food, drink and gifts for the dead in the hope that they would come and visit them.

When the Spanish started to arrive in the sixteenth century, they were offended by this pagan tradition and in particular by the morbid and gruesome art that accompanied it. Rather than ban it entirely however, they moved it to November 1st – All Saints Day in the Catholic calendar – and now the festival is a peculiar combination of Catholic celebrations and native Mexican traditions.

The Day of the Dead is celebrated all over Latin America, and takes different forms in each city and town. Mexico City, however, closes down for two whole days as the revelry takes over. November 1st is put aside to remember *las angelitos* – children who have died, and November 2nd is for commemorating adults. Shrines are built in homes, and families congregate in graveyards to watch over the lost ones.

Parades of ghoulishly dressed skeletons take over the streets, whilst macabre cakes and sweets shaped into skulls are handed out to children. Shops and streets are full of all manner of skeletons and other grotesque toys. Intricate tissue paper cut-outs called *papel picado*; elaborate wreaths and crosses decorated with paper or silk flowers; candles and votive lights fill market stalls.

It's a remarkable sight but chilling to see people bringing offerings to their dead to encourage them to revisit this earth. We were going to be doing an open air presentation in a park in the centre of the city on the day of this festival, but when it came to it, I felt strongly that we shouldn't be hiding away out of the limelight, but that we should be centre stage.

Taking a large gulp and praying hard, I approached the organisers of the main event taking place and asked if I could perform on their stage, and would you believe it, they said yes. Thirty minutes later I was performing one of the strangest gigs of my life – preaching to an enormous audience at the largest occult festival in South America, alongside a coffin and an assortment of weird people dressed in long black robes.

What an opportunity. I told the people who were there to think about their dead, that I knew the Lord of Life and that they could know Him too. I invited the huge crowd to ask Jesus to bring His light into their darkness – and over 300 people came forward. You could feel a little bit of heaven come to a very dark place that sunny afternoon. It was an awesome moment.

That's something that wouldn't have happened if I hadn't worked so hard to overcome my shyness. We could easily have stuck to the plan and had our little presentation in the corner of the park – we could still have patted ourselves on the back and congratulated ourselves on our evangelistic time in Mexico. But by pushing the boundaries, by stepping out of our comfort zone and taking a risk, we were able to have a much greater impact.

Jesus made it very clear that we should let His light shine and not hide it. We need to proclaim God's love from the hilltops. We need boldness to overcome our fear and faith to know that God is with us as we do it, and that it's He who will work in people's hearts as we share the Good News with them.

31

JUST FOR LAUGHS

Shopping isn't exactly my favourite occupation. So I was keen to be distracted one Saturday afternoon whilst out trailing around after my family. Out of the corner of my eye I noticed an earnest-looking chap in a black suit, with neatly combed hair, shouting about the Bible, so I decided to stop and listen in.

He looked like Roy Cropper, from *Coronation Street*, and had a line of six other 'brothers' behind him, each with a tidy side parting and looking equally earnest, clutching their black Bibles. Behind these dour gentlemen stood the 'sisters' in their head scarves and overcoats, looking as though they were auditioning for a part in some low budget Shakespearian tragedy.

I stood and watched for a while, listening to the doom and gloom they were communicating. After they'd finished their 'presentation' to an audience of one – yours truly – I felt I just had to go and say something.

I explained I was a Christian from a local church, and that I had a bit of experience when it came to presenting the Good News in the open air. I tried to be generously diplomatic as I attempted to make some subtle suggestions in terms of presentation. I felt it was important to try to communicate fun and life in presenting the Message, and gave them some pointers on understanding crowd dynamics.

I have been better received in a mortuary. The preacher asked me where it talked about crowd dynamics in the 'Word'. I resorted to what I do best in an awkward situation and decided it would be a good time to inject some humour to try to diffuse the tension. I replied that of course it didn't mention crowd dynamics in the Bible, but neither did it mention Jesus going to the toilet, and that, short of Jesus being plumbed differently to the rest of us, He probably did.

It turned out my humour was on a different level to the gentleman in front of me – if, that is, he had a sense of humour at all. He looked at me, lip curled in an incredible sneer, pointed at my colourful Swatch wristwatch, and declared loudly, 'Well, you can't be a real Christian wearing a watch like that.'

With that they all stormed off. (Home, I presume. Certainly not the pub.) I couldn't believe it. It wasn't very good news, and anyway what was wrong with my Swatch? Or my humour?

Actually, my humour got me into trouble on another occasion. I was over the moon a few years back when I got asked to co-host a weekly live LWT Sunday morning programme with TV favourite, the lovely Gloria Hunniford. What an honour to be asked and how fantastic to be on TV each Sunday sharing God with people.

Each programme was a live outside broadcast, which was nerve-racking but such a buzz, too. We had immense fun – working outdoors, interviewing people, presenting acts. One of my favourite memories is of interviewing a world champion sheep shearer and then trying to shear the sheep myself – not sure who looked more scared – me or the sheep. The night before the close shave, I'd lain awake in my hotel room, trying to learn sheep facts and genuinely worrying about the shearing, acutely aware that the normal suggestion for overcoming insomnia is to count sheep – but it wasn't really helping me.

The show was a great opportunity, though – the only Christian on the team, I was able to recommend all kinds of interesting people to appear: we had magicians and musicians, jugglers and record breakers. Above all, we presented Jesus in an attractive way and had fun whilst doing it.

Too much fun it seems; the day after the sheep shearing show I had a phone call from the producer telling me they were very sorry, but I was sacked. I was too much fun for religious TV. That was the end of my sparkling TV career – for the time being anyway. I was pretty devastated; especially when a little handwritten note came from Gloria saying that she was sorry it didn't work out. It made it even more final.

Nowadays, with hindsight, I'm quite chuffed. The fact is I am perfectly capable of being serious when I need to be and I can do solemn if the situation calls for it. But what I won't do is suck the joy out of Christianity. We are commanded to be joyful. 1 Thessalonians 5:16 tells us to *'be joyful always'*. Jesus was a charismatic character who drew people to Him. The message of the Gospels is Good News, meant for sharing, and we should smile whilst we tell it. After all, it would be wrong to keep it to ourselves.

Many people have a false perception of Christians, thinking they are a bunch of miserable spoilsports. Some people believe we spend our lives feeling guilty for having fun, and that the Bible is a book of rules and regulations that stop us from doing anything interesting.

The reality couldn't be more different. Choosing to follow Jesus is a decision to embark on an incredible adventure with the Creator of the world – the God who loves us beyond measure. The Good News is exactly what it says – so let's step out of the gloom, light the world up with the joy that we have been given and don't let anyone tell you that a Seiko is more spiritual than a Swatch.

32

THE FAME GAME

Over the years I've been fortunate enough to be given countless TV and radio opportunities. Escapology and magic tricks make less of an impact on radio, obviously, but I'm always one for a challenge. On TV I seem to have appeared on everything from *The Big Breakfast* to *The Disney Club*, with a couple of stints on *Songs of Praise* in between. Appearing like that is always great fun and a chance to make new friends, as well as, more importantly, to reach millions with the Christian message.

In 1999, I was invited to be part of a huge BBC production for the millennium, to be held in the National Indoor Arena in Birmingham. It was a schools event and 14,000 children were shipped in for a show that would go out on the telly a few weeks later. A major part of the programme was a focus on Third World debt, with the Jubilee 2000 campaign having a very high profile. I performed a death defying, upside down, strait jacket escape, dangling from the top of the venue to illustrate the idea of breaking the chains of injustice.

Over the course of the rehearsals and recordings, I became great pals with the presenters. We enjoyed meals out and the occasional nightcap back at the hotel. I was very intrigued to see how these well-known TV personalities coped with their success; how they handled fame and recognition everywhere they went. They were pretty accommodating most of the time, and seemed more than happy to pose for photos or sign dozens of autographs.

One particular morning, one of the presenters and I were enjoying breakfast in the hotel. Over our eggs and bacon I noticed I was losing his attention. Confident that my scintillating conversation couldn't possibly be at fault, I asked him what was on his mind. It transpired that he was somewhat distracted by the pretty waitress behind me, who kept looking over to our table.

This, he said, was one of the bonuses of being famous – he went on to brag about the dates he'd had, the phone numbers on his contact list, and he regaled me with the lurid details of his conquests. He then, excitedly, described in terms his dear old mum wouldn't have liked, his appreciation of the girl behind me.

'Watch this,' he said as he winked at her and motioned her towards him. He got his ever-ready pen from his pocket in anticipation of an autograph, and a twinkle in his eye at the hope of more. You should have seen his face when the young woman came over to the table, smiled at me and said, 'Are you Steve Legg?' – completely ignoring his twinkly-eyed presence in the process. In fact she didn't seem to know him from a bar of soap.

I was pretty surprised myself. It turned out that she had

become a Christian at a church event I had spoken at a few years before, and she wanted to say thank you. She said she had been living for Jesus for the last five years and accepting Christ had changed her life completely.

I was very touched. If I'm completely honest, I was also a little amused. I had quite enjoyed watching my celebrity companion's facial expression change as he realised he'd made a bit of an idiot of himself. After all, as will be patently obvious by now, whatever the situation it's usually *me* who has to try and cover my embarrassment. Mostly though, it made me think. What a peculiar world we live in – where success is so often measured by fame.

We live in a culture where children aspire simply to be 'famous' and people can become celebrities for the wrong reasons or for no reason at all. People measure success by all manner of inconsequential yard sticks and they spend their lives chasing after it. They devote their time to being seen in the right places, with the right people, in the right clothes, doing nothing of substance other than breathing.

Some have more noble pursuits – they want to be the fastest, strongest, the brightest or the most ruthless. They spend hours in the office, months in training and their weekends at the computer. At the end of the day, though, we need to sit back and think about what counts. Do we live our lives to be successful or do we want to be significant? Do we live our lives to honour ourselves or to honour God and those around us?

We can have a phenomenal impact on the people we meet – not just by dangling upside down from a rope and telling them about Jesus, but in the everyday things we do. When we live for God, we can profoundly influence people's lives.

I was touched by that waitress remembering me. I know most of the time I will never meet the people whose lives I have impacted. It's the same for all of us. We rarely do. But it's not about the recognition we will receive. Everywhere we go, we meet people and we can sow seeds. And occasionally, we may get to see the fruits of our labours.

More often, though, we don't – but that doesn't mean we should stop sowing. Let's live lives of significance – improve the world around us, be that through campaigning for social justice, serving the poor, preaching the Good News, befriending the lonely neighbour down the road or giving some real time to our family. Let's not do it for the recognition, the thanks or the reward. Let's do it because we're growing to be more like Jesus, and it's what He would have done.

After all, stars burn and fade, but God's Kingdom will last forever.

33

FREEBIE JEEBIES

I like to think of myself as a generous man. I love giving gifts to my wife, just little things like picking up donuts on my way home for a treat, or her favourite chocolate when I stop in the newsagents to buy myself a paper.

I get a real kick out of getting treats for my kids – even if it's just silly stuff like wrapping up the remote control and letting them be in charge of it for an evening. There isn't much I enjoy more than having people round for dinner and entertaining guests. Throughout the summer months, every Thursday night is barbecue city at my place.

But if there's one thing I can't bear, it's freeloaders. You know what I mean. It's the people who pull out their cheapest bottle of value lemonade (RRP around 19 pence) to bring to the home group barbecue and then spend the evening knocking back your treasured 1945 *Chateau Lafite Rothschild* like it's going out of fashion. It's not because they are struggling financially; they're just tight. At church we often prepare a hamper of food for newly weds. Everyone is asked to put something in. For a pretty wealthy church there is always a disproportionate number of tins of supermarket value baked beans.

People like to see what they can get away with. Recently we were at a large event – I shouldn't mention names so let's just say that it was a large exhibition of Christian resources. We had a stand for *Sorted* magazine – our new publication for blokes – and spent three days smiling at people, grabbing their attention, singing the magazine's praises and persuading people to sign up or buy some copies.

It's pretty exhausting stuff. It seems a bit lame, but when you're not used to it, standing around all day is harder than it looks. I'd so much rather be active and moving about. As my back started to throb, I think it's fair to say that my tolerance levels began to dip. The number of people who wanted to know if they could have a free copy started to irritate me. People would walk up to the stand and ask us what was free – they didn't really seem bothered about who we were or what we were actually trying to achieve.

Don't get me wrong. If we could afford to give *Sorted* away, we would – in fact we do. Thanks to the kindness of some incredibly generous Christians (there are plenty of those out there, too) – we give hundreds away. To be precise, we give over £2,500 worth away of each edition as a gift to the armed forces and prisons. But we need regular subscribers to fund this and to help the publication pay for itself as we continue to grow in remarkable ways.

There were people who came along to the stand and read

the magazine cover to cover without buying it. One guy stood for nearly an hour, chuckling away at the stories, getting absorbed in the articles before folding it back up, replacing it on the shelf and walking away. I mentioned that we weren't a library. He laughed, thinking I was kidding. I wasn't. Unbelievable.

Another interesting market was the pray-ers. We had a number of women come to see the stand who told us that their partners weren't Christians and that they were looking for man-friendly ways to get the Gospel to them. We suggested that they might like to take out a subscription for a Father's Day treat or buy a copy to take home for their significant other. 'I'll pray about it,' came the reply. It's £2.50, what's to pray about? I got sent for a coffee break before I completely morphed into my alter ego – Rick Spleen.

The icing on the cake, however, was a couple of very friendly ladies who showed an interest in the magazine. They chatted with Rebekah as she invited them to take a look. One of them spotted a Tim Vine interview and told us all about her husband's appreciation of the comedian. She explained that he often used a Tim Vine gag in his sermons and never missed his show on TV.

Rebekah suggested that she buy a copy of the magazine for her husband to enjoy. She smiled – and said she'd fetch him. Five minutes later she was back, husband in tow – and he was delighted to stand and read the article. He even jotted down a couple of gags before replacing the magazine neatly on the stand, grinning at Rebekah, saying, 'Very good,' and walking off. I don't often see my wife speechless but this was one of those times. It was almost worth it for the peace and quiet.

I don't mean to be uncharitable; I'd be the first to say that we should share what we have with those in need. Sometimes, though, I think that as Christians we expect a bit of an easy ride. We think that we have a direct line to the Miracle Maker and we expect Him to play along. We somehow expect *our* lives to be safe from the troubles that bother others; we think we should have a privileged life without really having to work that hard for it and we treat God like a celestial Jimmy Savile – out there to fix things for us.

It happens in many different areas of life. Teenagers pray the night before an exam, asking God to help them pass – but they haven't so much as picked up their books beforehand. Stressed parents beg God to make their children better behaved at school, but work all hours and never make time for their kids. We ask God to give us opportunities to spread the Gospel yet we never step outside our cosy little clique to see who is out there.

God is our wonderful, Heavenly Father who loves to give gifts to His children, but I firmly believe He expects us to walk on our own two feet. He has given us gifts to use. Being a Christian is not about having an easy ride, in fact Jesus assures us we will have troubles in this life, and God sometimes takes us along difficult roads in order for us to grow and learn. What we don't ever have to do is walk that road alone. God walks with us always – He goes before us in all that we do, and He promises never to leave or forsake us.

There is one road, though, that God has walked for us. In fact He sent His Son to take our place. God's greatest gift of all – the gift of life itself – is free to us, but it cost Him the most precious thing He had, His Son.

Jesus laid down His life for us – He knows what it is to do

things the hard way. Let's stop looking to get something for nothing, and never forget it's better to give than to receive. Let's unwrap the gifts God has given us, and put them to good use. Let's ask God to lead us forward, to walk with us all the way, but let's not ask Him to do everything for us.

And if you are ever stuck for a present for the man in your life – you know where to find us.

34

WHO DARES, SWIMS

I like to big things up. You may have noticed. One of my best
stunts has been escaping from a strait jacket whilst dangling
upside down from a 40 metre high crane. For a man who is not
that comfortable with heights, that's quite an achievement. I
was hoping to do the same thing from a helicopter and break a
world record, but the chopper we were going to use crashed
the week before and I had a change of heart. But when I talk
about what I do, I often describe my 'death defying' stunts and
suggest that I have no fear.

I told my wife when I met her that I wasn't afraid of
anything. We were having a kind of 20 questions over the
telephone right at the beginning of our relationship. I asked all
the typical men questions – what colour are your eyes? What
are your favourite flowers? (Obviously I scribbled down the
answers so that one day I could look amazing when I sent the
right ones.) Rebekah, in all her glorious womanhood, wanted

to know what things wake me up and leave me worrying in the middle of the night; what my ex-wife would say if she asked her why we broke up, and what I'm afraid of. Clearly, Rebekah learned the fine art of flirting in a far tougher place than I.

No man I know wants to tell a woman on a first date that he has any fears at all – we want to be big and manly and brave and powerful. We don't want to confess that we scream at the sight of a spider. (I don't incidentally, that was hypothetical.) We also do not want our prospective partner so much as to think about our ex, and we most definitely do not want to be the kind of person who has any reason at all for insomnia. So I said I was afraid of nothing.

Since then she has slowly come to realise that I may have been somewhat economical with my answer. On holiday, she and I had a romantic dinner overlooking the harbour; it was as we walked along, hand in hand, looking at the boats, with me keeping a good 20 feet from the edge, that I gave away my discomfort. I would like to point out that 'fear' is a very strong word; I'm just happier where I can't trip and fall to my death.

Similarly on honeymoon, we stayed at a beautiful hotel, with its own private beach and caves within which you can swim. Rebekah had explored whilst I was asleep in the sun, and woke me up to go and see. I took two steps down into the cave's mouth, said, 'Very good,' and turned round and walked back into the sun. It's not that I was scared, of course, just that I prefer to be in the sunlight.

A few years ago, my mate, Nick, and I were invited to Azle, Texas, to speak and perform at some churches there. It's a lovely part of the world situated on the shores of Eagle

Mountain Lake. We were looked after by our hosts, Paul and Perrianne Brownback, magnificently. The hospitality was phenomenal – amazing rooms, fantastic food and great friendship. We were there over Labour Day and Paul took us out for a trip on the lake – he had a little motor boat that belonged to his aunty.

We got into the boat and Paul struggled to get the motor working. Nick and I, not being motor boat experts by any stretch of our imaginations, kept our noses out, but we helped drag the boat out of the water when Paul said he thought it might start more easily if we pulled it onto the beach. He was right. The engine leapt to life and we pushed the boat back into the water, climbed in and set off. I felt like a real man, sailing out into the middle of this vast lake with my fishing rod.

Minutes later, my manliness had deserted me as we realised that there was smoke billowing from the engine. I started having flashbacks to my beloved Capri and wondered what the odds were of surviving two exploding vehicles.

Paul, never one to be alarmist, gave us a life jacket each and told us to jump if we thought the engine was about to explode. How do you know when an engine is about to explode? The guys in the lakeside restaurant where I'd been performing the night before seemed to be fairly sure – they were waving at us shouting, 'She's going to blow.' It felt like a scene from a horror movie where the hero stumbles from one nightmare into another.

I wanted to jump then and there but knew that swimming was not my forte and we were a very long way from the shore. Finally, the fear of the engine overcame the fear of the lake. Nick grabbed me by the hand and we jumped. I closed my eyes waiting for the impact of the water, but opened them fast as my feet jarred into solid ground. The water was no more than two feet deep – I'd have made more of a splash re-enacting my death defying leap into a paddling pool. I felt a little foolish as we slowly waded towards the shore.

So often our fears are blown out of all proportion; we worry about things that will never happen and we stress about outcomes we will never see. In the middle of the night fears come to haunt is – all the what-ifs taunt us with their possibilities. Sometimes we can spend so long worrying about what might happen that we lose track of what actually *is* happening. We worry about what will happen if we lose our jobs, if our child gets sick or worse. We worry about what will happen if we fail our exams or lose someone we love. Sometimes we worry about these things even when they're unlikely ever to happen.

In Matthew's Gospel, Jesus clearly told us *'not to worry about tomorrow, for tomorrow will worry about itself'*. That doesn't mean that we shouldn't plan for our future or take responsibility for the consequences of our actions. It means that we should take a day at a time and not get caught up in our fears for the future. We need to take control of the life that we are actually living, enjoy it to the full, face problems head on and deal with them as they occur. But let's not waste hours of our lives fretting about things that may never happen.

After all, the water may not be as deep as you think.

35

MAKING CHRISTMAS HIS STORY

Those who know me will have heard me tell this story many times. It's a tale that turned my life around whilst setting me on a path of more stress and sleepless nights than was good for me. It changed the direction of the work that I did and made me step into a whole new realm of outreach and faith; learning new skills, meeting new people and raising more money than I thought possible.

It was a little boy who did it. I don't even know his name. I didn't actually meet him. He could just be an urban myth. But he, whoever he is or isn't, made quite an impact on me. The story goes that there was a little boy in school whose teacher told him and his classmates an account of the Nativity at Christmas. It was the first time that the boy had heard it and at the end of the lesson he hung back in the classroom. The teacher asked him whether he had enjoyed the day. 'I did,' he said. 'I really loved the story about Jesus.' But he stopped and looked puzzled and the teacher asked why. 'I just don't get why Mary and Joseph named their little boy after a swear word,' was his reply.

Well, the story hit me for six. I didn't grow up in a Christian family but I'd always known the Christmas story. I was flabbergasted that people wouldn't. Then I overheard one of the mums in the playground bemoaning the fact that her child had been given a part in the nativity play, and she'd realised she had never actually told them the 'Jesus part' of Christmas, just the 'Father Christmas part'. I decided to look into it some more.

I discovered that there were over 12.5 million children in the UK but that only 756,000 of those went to church on Sunday. That meant that over 11.5 million children didn't. That's 11.5 million children who might never hear the 'Jesus part' of Christmas. I had to do something about it. I wanted to give Jesus to children all over the country at Christmas. More than that really, I knew that God was asking me to do it – that the reason that this story had grabbed my attention was because God was shouting it out to me.

And with that, *It's a Boy!* was born. It started life as a Christmas card, developed into a musical play for schools, an award-winning book and eventually a cartoon that took a fresh look at the birth of Jesus through the eyes of three quails – a bird's eye view of the greatest story in human history.

I found an amazing Christian animator called Julian Tewkesbury. He was an incredible find and he assembled a fantastic team – the very best we could afford. Julian's sister, Alexa, did a phenomenal job writing the screenplay and next we needed a cast. I persuaded some well-known personalities to provide the voices. Squeaky-voiced comedian, Joe Pasquale, played the inn-keeper; Cannon and Ball were a couple of the quails, and friends from *The Bill*, *Casualty* and *Spooks* played other important roles. Steven Berkoff was a special guest star playing King Herod. Over a glass of wine at a Christians in Entertainment soirée, I even chatted up Sir Cliff Richard who agreed to sing the title track. It was hard to believe the remarkable cast that had fallen into place.

All I had to do now was to find £250,000 to fulfil the dream. It doesn't sound much if you say it quickly, but if I'm honest, it almost killed me. I hit the road and shared my heart and my vision. What started as a six-month project took three years to complete. Gifts from 50 pence to £50,000 came in over that period as I stepped out and never lost faith in the vision.

The production was beset with problems from day one. The editing of the movie was the biggest killer of all. When a scene is assembled in the editing software, it has to be 'rendered' so that it will actually play on the computer. Julian's computer was everything that it should be and had plenty of space – but it kept crashing; what should have taken a couple of days took weeks.

Other machines crashed unexpectedly, and one catastrophe seemed to follow another. Even Stansted airport was fog-bound the night the master was due to leave for manufacture in Austria. When it did finally arrive there 24 hours late, it was delivered to the wrong address causing more hassle, more worry and more significant delays. It really was a battle from start to finish.

But at last, after three years of blood, sweat, tears – hope, faith and belief – on Sunday 27th November 2005, we finally unveiled the cartoon at a packed premiere at the world famous Odeon Cinema in London's Leicester Square. There was a red carpet, crowd barriers, stretch limousines, TV crews and hordes of photographers.

Then, amidst all the buzz and expectation, over 850 children, adults, celebrities and VIPs began to arrive to pack the cinema and enjoy the film. It truly was one of the best days of my life. But the really exciting part didn't begin until the following day – when a copy of the DVD was sent free of charge to all 25,199 primary schools in the UK – a potential audience of nearly six million children.

And the rest, as they say, is history. It was an incredible time for me – I learnt so much. Not just the nuances of computer animation, but big personal lessons. I learnt so much more about faith. I said earlier that I had to raise £250,000. When the project started, we actually thought it would cost £20,000 and take six months. The figure escalated enormously as new technologies became involved, computers gave up and other trials came blasting through. But I thank God that it started small, because when it began, that's what I had faith for.

I don't know what my reaction would have been right at the beginning if I had have known quite what an enormous project it was going to be, but I think, if I'm honest I would have thought it was too big. God is good; He never asks too much of us. He asked me to trust Him for £20,000 and I could manage that, so I got going and He provided.

Slowly as I gained confidence that God would provide, as I learnt the power of faith – I could trust Him for more. Though times were hard, though there were nights when I lay awake worrying, though computers crashed, flights were delayed and masters were lost, I was able to know that I trusted a God who provides and who keeps His promises.

It's a lesson I'll never forget. Walking in faith, depending on God, can feel frightening. Handing over the reins to Him and releasing the control on our lives can go against the grain of how we've lived for so long. But the rewards are phenomenal. The joy of watching God provide, the thrill of seeing Him move mountains and the honour of working with Him as He does it more than outweigh the discomforts of giving up our independence. So let's trust God in the small things as we learn to give Him control of everything that we do.

36

GHOST-FLUSTERS

Sometimes I wish I was still a child. I know my memories are probably rose-tinted, but it seems such a happy time. Kicking a football about with my mates, hanging out at the beach, playing pranks on one another. Halcyon days, before responsibilities came crowding in; a carefree time when life was all about fun.

Primary school, for me, was wonderful, particularly the final year when we were the eldest in school. We were the big kids and we lorded it over everyone else in the playground – rulers of all we surveyed. As the summer came and with it the prospect of all going to different senior schools, my band of mates stuck together and made all kinds of pacts to be friends forever. With one last glorious week before school finished for the summer, we were taken by our teachers to Leeson House.

A grade II listed building, this beautiful old manor house is located about a mile from Swanage in Dorset. It stands in gorgeous grounds and we were all set for a fantastic week. I was sharing a room with my best pals, Gavin Herbert and Richard Burfoot, and we were planning on having the holiday of a lifetime.

A guided tour around the house on our first evening there gave us all the history of the building. Once in our rooms that night, however, we extended the history and made it our own. Ghost stories are, after all, what school trips are all about and Leeson House was the perfect setting – all creepy corridors and creaking floorboards.

All was well until the lights went out and we were told to sleep. Tossing and turning in our beds, thoughts of unsettled spirits, headless horsemen and vengeful lords started to race through our heads. It began to bother us that we were sleeping in the bedroom the guide had said was haunted. Swapping ghost stories was an exciting adventure, but now things seemed more sinister as we wriggled further and further down beneath the endless sheets and scratchy blankets.

As is the way with children, we eventually started to drift off to sleep. Conversations became fewer and slower. Gav cut off half-way through a sentence and Richard was just replying in grunts. I closed my eyes and curled up, ready to give in to the tiredness – just as the wardrobe door swung open with an eerie creak.

Suddenly abandoning all thoughts of sleep, we sat bolt upright in our beds staring at the source of the scary noise. There, in the open doorway of the wardrobe, hovered a headless, white, ethereal body. We shrank back into our beds, screaming with fear as we pulled the sheets up over our noses. Absolutely terrified, we peered out of the top watching the shape as it swung gently, screaming once again while it shivered in front of us.

After what felt like hours, the door to the room flew open, this time with an almighty crash, and in burst our teacher, Mr Stark. He clicked on the lights and gave us the biggest telling off of our short, miscreant careers.

Uninterested in what had caused the fuss, he gave us a short, sharp lecture on what was an acceptable noise level and what would happen to us if we exceeded it again. His warning washed over us somewhat as we looked at him for as long as was necessary before turning our eyes back to the wardrobe.

We were astonished and not a little relieved to discover the 'ghost' had morphed into Gavin's dressing gown. It transpired that, in his haste, he had turned it inside out and hung it up on a hanger in the wardrobe, according to the strict rules we were following. Its white lining floated, emulating the phantoms we had talked about earlier.

A little abashed, we said, 'Sorry sir,' and promised to be quiet as mice. After Starky had gone, we pushed a chair up against the wardrobe to be totally safe and then snuggled back in our beds ready to sleep in peace.

It's amazing the way the mind works. In the full light of day it was obvious that the spectre was nothing more than a piece of clothing, but in the dark, after an evening of ghost stories, the dressing gown had taken on a far darker guise. The power of suggestion is phenomenal and can turn the most innocent of situations into something sinister.

By spending our time thinking about ghosts and headless

monsters, we had all but told our minds to expect to see them. So we didn't stop and use our common sense, or get out of bed and test the situation – we sat and screamed, getting more and more frightened by the minute.

It's called self-fulfilling prophecy; a long name for something simple. Setting out an expectation and seeing it happen, because it's what we presume we'll see. An example is, when a new teacher tells a class they have heard they are disruptive and poor at maths – and then they are. How much better if that same teacher said they heard the class was well-behaved and looked forward to seeing how good they were at maths? What a difference that would make.

It's such an easy thing to do – we judge situations quickly and set our expectations even before we meet people. We often sum them up from our first impression, not really allowing them to be anything other than what we have already decided.

Our words have incredible power and we need to take responsibility for them. The things that we speak into other people's lives can have a profound effect, so we need to stop and think before we open our mouths. In the book of James we read that, '*A word out of your mouth may seem of no account, but it can accomplish nearly anything – or destroy it*'. So let's choose our words carefully. Let's speak with purpose to those around us, and let's be people who encourage and bring out the best in those we meet.

And always check the contents of the wardrobe before you scream.

37

RINGING IN MY EARS

It was my fifteenth anniversary. Fifteen years since I'd first hung up my banker's shoes and joined a Pioneer TIE – Training In Evangelism – Team for a year. It truly was life-changing and is an important date for me. Every 3rd October marks another year that God has kept me and given me the honour to work for Him and see what He can do in people's lives. It's not quite a cake and champagne day, however – certainly not on my fifteenth anniversary. Instead, I was up at 3:00 in the morning and on the road to Norwich for a breakfast meeting and harvest service.

Having left so early, I was delighted to have learned that the church was providing breakfast before the service. Bleary-eyed I arrived, spruced up, tucked into my bacon sandwich and then spoke at the church's harvest celebration. We had a good time and afterwards I set off, heading for an evening service that I was taking on the other side of town. I took my time, stopped in a pub for a spot of lunch, and then consulted my directions for the next venue.

It's time for a little aside. I need to say that all this took place BSN. Before Sat Nav. I'm not being sponsored by any of the producers, it is just true – I love Satellite Navigation. One of the banes of my life has been the odd directions that I have been sent over the years, where one false instruction, one blink at the wrong time, leaves you hopelessly lost in an alien environment. I have lost track of the times I have been lost. There is nothing more dangerous than driving through suburbia in the pitch black, with a handwritten map on the seat by your side trying to find your way to a remote church hall in the middle of nowhere. The arrival of Sat Navs is akin to the discovery of the wheel. It has revolutionised my life.

Anyway, my directions on this fateful day seemed quite clear. I followed them, without mishap, all the way to the correct road. I relaxed knowing that the worst was over and consulted the last direction. I needed to drive past the front of the church, go round the back to find the car park and then I could go on in. I was assured that whilst the church looked small, it was much larger on the inside. Like the Tardis.

I found the church car park and discovered a coned off space – saved just for me. What hospitality. In true male fashion, I was desperate for the toilet so I sprinted in through the back door and smiled at the guy who was waiting to greet me. He shook my hand as I asked him to point me in the direction of the toilets. Relieved, I came back and said hello properly and explained that I was there to speak. My new friend was delighted. He gave me a guided tour of the building – which truly was vast on the inside and super-modern – and asked me what time I was on.

He explained that there was a service on at the moment but that I was free to wander round and make myself at home. This I did. I stuck my head through the door to the main chapel and listened to the speaker for a couple of minutes. He was American and it occurred to me that we had a very different style. It was all rather formal. Everyone was suited and booted and I was there in jeans and a t-shirt.

Elsewhere in the building there was a basketball court, offices and a number of classrooms with hundreds of children. It struck me as a little unusual not to find any crosses or murals anywhere, but I thought not too much more of it.

As no one had offered me coffee or a cup of tea, I wandered upstairs to find somewhere quiet to sit, and found a room with some desks and chairs and interesting machines. As I sat down I investigated further, and discovered that what I was looking at were microfiche machines – jam-packed full of people's genealogies.

Slowly the cogs started whirring in my brain. I was in the wrong church. I'd ended up in a Mormon chapel. And that meant that I most definitely was not 'on' at 6:30. I picked myself up, snuck back downstairs to find my friend from earlier waiting – still in the foyer. He coughed as I arrived and told me he was terribly sorry, but it appeared I had parked in the space they reserved for a disabled member. I mumbled an apology, got into my car and made my hasty escape to the venue where I should have been all along, a few hundred metres up the road. I'd not only got the wrong church, I'd gone and got the wrong religion. What a muppet.

Talk about a Tardis. It was a totally reality-bending experience. Doctor Who hasn't a patch on me. I'm just glad my alarm bells started ringing before they had me in a suit, being baptised on behalf of my granny and married to three wives.

Alarm bells are pretty important things and we ignore them at our peril. I was exaggerating – I'm quite sure the worst that would have happened is that I would have ended up confused and embarrassed, which is a pretty common experience for me. But we need to be on our guard. It is very easy to end up in situations that we shouldn't be in, whether that is in our relationships, our careers, our conversations or even our theology.

We know when it's happening – we've all had the pangs of conscience that prick at us, telling us to take care, like God poking us with a stick to try and get our attention. We've all ignored them, too, and carried on regardless. It's not a good idea. When we start to ignore our alarm bells, we start to become deaf to them. They slowly become white noise that blurs into the background, and then we end up in situations that aren't good for us.

God is our loving Heavenly Father, who wants the best for us. He wants to keep us out of danger and tries to protect us from getting hurt. As we listen to His voice, we will start to recognise it more clearly. So let's listen to God when He speaks to us – through our conscience, through our friends and through His Word. Let's heed His warnings and keep ourselves safe.

After all, you wouldn't want to wake up one day to realise you've got three mother-in-laws.

38

ONE FOOT IN THE GRAVE

What with one thing and another, I've had two months off from the gym. That, combined with the Christmas period, our honeymoon, and generally just enjoying my food, means that I'm not as trim as I was. I hadn't thought much about it, but various friends had taken it upon themselves to comment. 'Marriage is clearly suiting you'; 'You're enjoying the home cooking I see'; and, far more to the point, 'You've piled it on, haven't you?' – have all come my way. Don't get me started on why people think it's OK to say these things to a man – they wouldn't dream of saying them to a woman – otherwise they'd get a bunch of fives.

So I'm back at the gym. Hardcore – every day. I even get up early at the weekend and I'm running miles each day pushing myself a little further each time. I want to shed those pounds and impress those people who have noticed the weight go on.

If they could see me now, though, I'm not sure how impressed they'd be. Everything hurts. If they could watch me gently lowering my aching body into bed amidst the burning aroma of 'deep-heat', they'd be even less so. I hurt my ankle running so I switched to the cross trainer. I don't know what I did on that, but now my knee sends sharp signals to my brain every time I try to sit down. I think it's shin splints. No, take a check on that – I've just googled running injuries and am sure that I'm actually suffering from runner's knee – *and* shin splints.

On top of this, I have no idea what I have done to my shoulders, but when I went to kiss my wife goodnight last night, it felt as if someone had stabbed me in the back. Twice. Grimacing as your wife kisses you is not a good idea I can assure you and tends to lead to more pain. She most definitely is not impressed with my gym antics – no matter how much I tell her that I'm doing it all for her.

Finally, this morning as I got out of bed, a feat even more painful than getting into it, I groaned and said, 'Oh, I ache all over, darling.' And, through the mists of time, came the echo of my father saying, 'These old bones of mine.' I've turned into my dad. As he gets in and out of his chair, he groans and tells us about his old bones. I'll be saying 'I'm not as young as I was' next. I already have parties that the neighbours don't complain about and that, whilst clearly a neighbourly thing, makes me feel old.

I've got a distinct pride in my lawn mower. It used to be an expensive thing that you had to own to stop your garden from getting out of control – but now I get a lot of satisfaction from getting proper stripes on my lawn, and I spend time trimming the edges making sure they're just right. I've even been known to admire other people's lawns – you know – ones with no moss, daisies and proper 'premium green' turf.

Then there's the fact that when they talk about the credit crunch on TV, I know what they're on about – I understand what hedge funds are and I know what equity means. Back when I was young I would have glazed over. I haven't been on a course in investment terms; I've just picked up the information in the university of life.

I don't like some of the music my kids are into, but I restrain myself from saying that it's got no tune and is just noise, only because that would be leaping another generation and I would be turning into my gran. But some days, I reckon I can understand her a little better now. I'm feeling a bit old and past it. I'm just waiting to see my favourite childhood toys on the *Antiques Roadshow*. It hasn't happened yet, but let's face it – I'm watching the *Antiques Roadshow*. That says it all. Although if I ever start enjoying *Last of the Summer Wine* you have permission to shoot me.

Now, I know you're all skipping to my picture on the back cover and thinking I can't possibly be that old. You're right, I'm not – I've only just gone 40, but I still have days when I wonder if my time has been and gone. I have moments when I think that someone younger could do my job better; perhaps connect with kids more easily – maybe my skills are a bit passé. Jesus, after all, had done everything by the time He was 33.

The thing is, I'm not Jesus. I'm me. Whatever gifts God has given me are there for me to use for as long as He gives me breath. Things do change. My life has taken all kinds of different directions. Working with *Sorted* magazine takes up a huge amount of my time nowadays and I haven't dangled from a crane in years – my shin splints wouldn't allow it. Throughout it all, however, God is still with me.

Look at some of the characters in the Bible. Moses was 80 when he led the Israelites out of Egypt and across the Red Sea. Caleb was 85 when he took the land of Mount Hebron from the fearful Anakim. Even according to the most conservative estimates, Noah floated his boat aged 50. These guys had probably got aches and pains. They probably didn't get down with the kids, but there is no doubt whatsoever that God used them mightily.

God isn't restricted by age or infirmity. His power transcends all the barriers that we perceive. One of the most moving things I have ever watched is a video clip of *Team Hoyt*. You may have seen it. Dick and Rick Hoyt are father and son. Rick is a quadriplegic with cerebral palsy. At birth, the umbilical cord was wrapped around his neck and his parents were told he would never walk or talk or understand what was going on around him. But they persisted, always kept him part of the family and eventually, as technology improved, taught him to communicate through a computer.

Rick told his dad that he wanted to do a sponsored run to raise money for a local athlete who had been paralysed in an accident. They ran it together – Dick pushing Rick's wheelchair. They came second to last. But Rick said that he had felt, for the first time, as though he wasn't handicapped. Dick, aged 40 and afraid of water, started training. They have now completed well over 65 marathons, 81 half marathons and 950

iron man events, triathlons and the like. Dick is 68 yea[rs]
and still running strong.

These men – one disabled and one nearly 70 – inspire
people all over the world. They use their story to promote the
integration of disabled people into everyday life and use their
experience to tell people about God. Neither age nor infirmity
has hindered God working through them. And it needn't with
us – we might think that we are too old, past it or just plain
tired, but God sees deeper within. He sees the treasure that He
has buried within us and He wants to let it shine.

Moses, Caleb and Noah probably all thought they were
past it, in fact we know they questioned God's wisdom
choosing them at times. Perhaps this is what made them who
they were. They knew they had to rely on His strength, so they
did – the results are recorded in the annals of history.

When we feel old, when we feel tired and incapable let's
remember that we have a God who is working on the inside –
in 2 Corinthians 4 we are reminded that though we are
*'outwardly wasting away, inwardly we are being renewed day by
day'*. Our bodies may grow weak, but our spirits, if we let them,
just get stronger.

We may have one foot in the grave but the other walks on
holy ground.

39

SILENCE IS GOLDEN

Back in the golden years – the years before children, frightening mortgages and having to think about my waistline, I used to frequent the Rustington Sports and Social Club with other mates from church. It was at the end of my road – just perfect for popping in for a swift half with my pal, Ishy.

It's important that you get a full picture of the delight that was the club. It was hardly an executive lounge – more of a scene from the Wild West. A real spit and sawdust place. As you sat with your beer, you half expected to see the door blow open and tumbleweed dance across the floor – if it didn't stick to it that is. The amount of beer that had been spilt on the wooden floor was beyond measure. People had been known to walk straight out of their shoes.

It's the kind of place you go to get a good solid pint rather than a fancy pants cocktail. They'd look at you odd if you asked for a gin and tonic – as though you'd got a little above yourself.

If you asked for a wine spritzer, they'd wipe the dust off the bottle and give it a shake.

There was a classier side – the lounge bar. The only difference was that it had carpet on the floor. There was a long bar where most people stood, but around the edge there were tables and chairs – red velour to hide the spills. It wasn't class but it was ours. Our local. I even had my own glass – with my name on it. You couldn't fault the hospitality. If you had so much as a centimetre of beer left in your glass and took it to Merv behind the bar to ask him to put a half in, he'd always fill it to the top – a Sussex half he called it. Merv was a right gent.

Ishy and I popped in most evenings to show our support. As a church many of us went up after home group – there could be over 100 of us there, having a drink and enjoying each other's company. They were good times. It wasn't posh, it wasn't hard work, it was just friendship and being part of our community.

One Bank Holiday Monday, there were about a dozen of us from church up at the club, having a beer and a laugh. It was a busy night – there must have been over 200 people there in all. After a couple of beers, my mates, Chris and Scott, got up to go to the toilet. Just as they left the room, the club's steward, Robin, coughed and asked us to stand for a two-minute silence for Peter Rolfe, the club President, who had died the previous week. Peter was a great guy, so we all stood, bowed our heads and paid our respects to the President.

All of us rose to our feet, bar Chris and Scott, who had heard none of this as they were still in the gents. They were still laughing over whatever it was we were talking about before they'd gone, like girls, in a pair to the toilet. And they were still laughing when they came back out – and stopped dead in their tracks at the sight before them.

I have never seen anything like it. Their smiles froze as they came face to face with the parallel reality they seemed to have entered. They had left a rowdy pub in the middle of Happy Hour and seemed to have returned, only minutes later to an enormous prayer meeting – 200 people standing in perfect silence with their heads bowed.

I watched as their faces slipped from grins to consternation, like ice cream melting and sliding down a child's chin. I had to swallow my laughter as I watched them choking back their own. Their bewildered expressions as all 200 people turned to see who was disturbing the peace were priceless. They swiftly caught the mood and dropped their heads – mostly to avoid the stares from the room.

Silence is a funny, thing. I, personally, with six children and a wife with a propensity for chatter, value it highly. I know others find it very uncomfortable – Rebekah for starters. When we were first getting to know each other, it took her a while to learn that me not chattering away wasn't a sign of disinterest, it was just me.

She still tells with horror one of her worst teaching stories – not the child who came into class totally drunk, not the child who hit her with a belt – not even the child who came in to her lesson with a BB gun. No, one of Rebekah's worst moments was in her first school, a private school in Kenya, where on Speech Day the staff were required to sit on the stage facing the school and parents for over two hours. Keeping her mouth closed and not fidgeting for so long nearly broke her.

But silence is important. It's not until the noise calms down and the distractions stop that we can truly listen. When I've spoken about friendship evangelism, one of the things that I point out to people is that we have two ears and one mouth, and that we should use them in that order. People like to be listened to. We need to know what questions they have – not just fire random information at them and answer questions they're not asking.

In our relationships we can get so caught up in the busyness of lives, so lost in the chatter, that we miss the signals that are being sent out by the person we love. We stop listening to them and just keep talking, oblivious to what they are trying to say.

The place where I notice this most of all though, is with God. We get so good at praying that we forget that prayer is a conversation – a two-way dialogue. Or at least it should be. We're great at asking God for things; we're good at thanking Him for what He's done; we're pretty practised at praising Him, too, but stopping and listening?

We need to have moments of quietness to allow God to speak into our hearts. In the Book of Kings, God sent Elijah to the mountains to spend time with Him. There was a mighty wind, an earthquake and a fire and God was not in any of these, but in the silence that followed, Elijah heard God speak – in a still, small voice.

Thunder and lightning, writing on the wall – these things all have their place, but the reality is that God speaks to our hearts in a soft voice. God should not have to shout to get our attention; we should actively listen to what our Father has to say. We need to create moments of peace, when we tune out the noise of our day. We need to stop talking, if just for a few minutes and listen to the One who loves us most.

After all, if He can't speak to us in the quiet, He will have to shout through the noise – and that can be pretty uncomfortable.

40

COUNT YOUR BLESSINGS

I have to confess to having the occasional bad day. Nothing horrific – just those days when it feels as though you should have stayed in bed. We all have days like it – days when the kids use up all the milk before you've had time to make yourself a morning cup of coffee; days when the person before you turns the toaster up a level and you don't realise and burn your toast. Then you discover – it was the last bit of bread. Burnt toast and black coffee bode badly in the morning.

   Today was one of those days. Not only did I have burnt toast and black coffee, but there was a new jar of marmalade. This sounds good – I could, after all, have discovered that too had run out. I wished it had. For some reason I cannot fathom, my wife had bought chunky marmalade. Who invented that? If I wanted little bits of leather in my jam, I would cut up my shoes and spread that on my bread.

It gets worse. I dropped the kids at school, and dashed to the gym to discover that a new jobsworth had joined the café. Whereas in the past I'd smile at the girl behind the till and she would let me have an early bird cup of free coffee (even though I was two minutes past the nine o'clock deadline), this new woman was clearly a signed up officer of the clock police – 'I'm terribly sorry, sir, but it has gone past nine o'clock.' Somehow, politeness is very irritating in these situations.

I survived the gym, coffeeless, in protest. I got over the indignity of realising that I was on the treadmill next to super gym man; a guy years older than me, half my weight and running at twice my speed whilst barely breaking into a sweat.

Having started after him, and feeling somewhat inadequate, I felt it was important not to get off the machine before him, so I kept up my pace and steeled myself to beat the ageing 'ironman'. He was wearing tiny shorts slashed up the side and a running vest, and I think he was running the marathon – I'm not sure which one, the geography is immaterial, the fact is he just wasn't stopping. And I was slowly seizing up. Ten miles later, I'd lost almost half my body weight in sweat and pulled something in my groin.

Red-faced and with a heart rate of 184 beats per minute, I staggered back to the changing room where I showered, dressed and turned my phone on. As ten messages flashed simultaneously on the screen, I realised I had a meeting an hour ago. It was for a radio interview – the chap was coming to my house with his wife – they'd driven 100 miles to see me – and had been sitting in the car outside for the duration of my mini marathon. Mortified, I dashed home to find them in their Fiat Punto, completely obscured by the condensation on the windows from their prolonged wait. That pretty much set the tone for the day.

Later that evening, we were taking the kids to church to see Watoto – an African children's choir. I was pretty keen to get out of it if I could. I just wanted to sit in some peace, rest my weary limbs, with a newspaper and a cup of coffee with milk in it. When our neighbour, Suzie, asked if we had a spare ticket, I managed the ultimate man multi-task – my heart leapt with joy whilst my face registered nothing of my inward glee. Rebekah said she could take the girls and I could have the evening off – it became almost impossible to hide the glee. Until that is, the girls shot me their best lost puppy dog looks and that was the end of that – I put my shoes on.

Watoto is the Swahili word for children. These children have all been orphaned – through AIDS and through war. All of them have lived through incredible hardship. Some, born into Northern Uganda's civil war, have been forced into becoming child soldiers and made to kill their neighbours. Some have even been ordered to kill their own parents.

One little girl spoke of how, after her mother died in childbirth, she and her brother had gone to live in the bush and had dug in the dust to find food. They are all children who have lost their parents, they have all been alone and they have all lived in terrible fear.

Watoto is also the name given to the project to which these children now belong. The vision of a church in Kampala, it already provides a home and family for 1,700 children and it hopes to extend this to cover 10,000 in the next ten years.

Children are placed in families with seven other children and a 'parent' to love them. They stay in these families for the rest of their lives. They are given an education, they are taught the love of Jesus, and they are supported as they grow into adults.

I was glad I went. These children are amazing. They danced and sang with the rhythm and enthusiasm that you only find in Africa, and they did it with the most beautiful smiles on their faces. These children, these *watoto*, who have known such sadness, were literally shining with the joy they have found in their new lives, their new families, but most of all in Jesus.

Watching them was a bit of a kick in the pants. I love the way God uses His celestial megaphone some days to get the message over. Here was me feeling sorry for myself, because I'd had a pants day, and now I was confronted with these youngsters, who had known hardship beyond my worst nightmares, telling me, a fully grown adult, that I should be thankful for all that He does for me.

Back home, there's a game we play with our children when they start grumbling about things not being fair. Rebekah will sit them down when they complain that they're bored, we're mean and the world is out to get them. Instead of arguing with them she asks them to tell her five good things about the day. The first thing is usually a struggle and needs a bit of suggestion, but by number five they get competitive and we often get up to ten good things before, with a smile, they acknowledge the world is not such a bad place.

It's called counting your blessings. The beautiful Watoto children taught me once again to praise God in every situation and they reminded me, too, that there is no situation so dark, where God's light cannot shine. There is no hole so deep that God cannot reach in and lift us out.

Watoto quoted Psalm 113 – '*He picks up the poor from out of the dirt, rescues the wretched who've been thrown out with the trash*'. We have an amazing, transformational God who delights in turning our world around – in rescuing us from our dark places, turning on the light and giving us joy.

Let's not dwell on our difficulties and wallow in our grief. Instead, let's call on the God who loves us, hold out our hands to Him and let Him lift us to a place where we can bask in the light of His love.

41

IN HOT WATER

Travelling up and down the country I'm always on the lookout for amusing diversions. I saw something on the side of a builder's truck that made me chuckle the other day. The company was called 'Singh and Singh Construction' and their slogan read – *'You've had the cowboys now hire the Indians'*. It almost makes me want to change my nationality and occupation and use it myself.

I've come across some teeth sucking, head shaking builders in my time, but given my general inadequacies with all things DIY, I've gradually accumulated a decent circle of tradesmen who I get to undertake jobs around the house. Instead of mastering the art of putting up the perfect shelf, I have turned into quite the barista – the best guy at making tea and coffee in the area. To be fair, it's pretty easy – strong tea with five sugars is the regulation beverage for any man who works with a tool belt and power drill.

I've become pretty good mates with Nick, the guy who can fix anything. Over the years, he has fitted my kitchen, laid my floor and built my shelves. He even climbed through a tiny window and rescued Maddie when she locked herself in the bathroom and we couldn't get the lock undone. Nick really can do everything, and do it so well that I've come to the conclusion there's very little point in my starting a job when I know how much better he'll do it in half the time.

A while ago, Nick had been fitting a new bathroom in our house. He'd all but finished and we were fully functional, but there were a couple of trims he still needed to complete the job. He said he'd pop round some time when he'd managed to get hold of the required pieces. A couple of days later, he did just that – he called round one evening when I was on the phone – praying.

Well, I wasn't praying, a friend at the other end of the line was. He was praying for me and my ministry, my family and every other sphere of my life. My pal, Liam, rings me up every now and again, always short of credit and asks me to call him back. I invariably do, because I love talking with him – or listening to him, at any rate. He's a laugh a minute Scouser who speaks faster than Rebekah – it's impossible to get a word in edgewise. When our time is nearly up, he inevitably winds up a sentence with, 'Let me pray for you, Ste', and launches into it. It's great, the ease with which our two-way conversation becomes a three-way one, with God in on the chat, too.

This particular evening, however, it got me into hot water. I was caught mid-prayer when Nick arrived, and seeing that I was on the phone, went on up to the bathroom. I didn't quite know how to get Liam to halt the prayer to tell Nick that actually my wife was in the bath. To be honest I'm not sure I registered the fact that fast. He was up the stairs and pushing the door open as it dawned on me that now was not the moment to be sealing the sink.

The screams, first feminine and then masculine as Nick got the shock of his week, were enough for me to call my phone prayer time to a halt with a speedy 'Amen', and run upstairs to face the wrath of my wife.

I bumped into a red-faced and mumbling Nick half-way down the stairs and apologised for failing to warn him, but he was out of the front door before I could finish. My wife's fury, however, wasn't going anywhere. It didn't seem the moment to point out that we do have a lock on the door that could have been used, or even that it was very early in the day to be having a bath. I just stumbled around trying to answer the question, 'What on earth was so important that you couldn't stop and tell Nick to come back later?'

The fact was that I didn't have a good answer. Prayer is important, obviously, but I'm quite sure that God would have understood me interrupting. In fact, had I not been so busy listening to Liam praying, I may have heard God shouting at me that I needed to stop Nick in his tracks. Prayer is a conversation like any other. It's a vital part of our Christian life. But it's not separate from the rest of our life.

It's good to have quiet time alone with God on a regular basis, to give Him some 'quality time'. It's right to try and protect this time, but there will be occasions when other things break in and take priority. What's the good of getting so caught up in being spiritual that we stop seeing the needs of those around us?

It's easy to get immersed in the rituals of our faith. We can get comfortable with the routines of our Christian life, believing them to be vital to our relationship with God. They are, but God walks with us in our everyday things. He's with us in our work place; He's with us as we travel and He's with us in our home. He's not restricted to our quiet times and our church times – He's with us in everything we do.

To be honest, I think the reason I didn't stop the prayer wasn't because I was worried about what God would think, it was because I didn't want to stop Liam mid-flow. That can often be the real reason we carry on with our spiritual activities – oblivious to what's going on around us. We go to church on a Sunday morning because we're concerned people will think we're slacking if we're not there.

Jesus got into hot water himself – by doing the right thing. He was healing people on a Sabbath – something the religious observers said He shouldn't do, and they criticised Him heavily for it. Jesus, though, was pretty clear in how He answered them. He knew that the law said you should rest on the Sabbath but He pointed out He was doing good, not evil, and it was in keeping with the spirit of God's law.

God doesn't want to be kept in a special little box – brought out for spiritual moments – He wants to be part of it all. Let's not separate our lives into spiritual and secular; let's not be so heavenly minded we're of no earthly use. Instead let's join heaven and earth, and see the impact that has on the people around us.

Perhaps it's also worth remembering that old adage, there's no point locking the bathroom door after the deeply embarrassed plumber has bolted.

42

CUSHTIE

I mentioned earlier that my wife calls me Del Boy; it's not really a term of endearment. The first time she gave me the name was when we had just started dating and I had cut a phone conversation with her short to watch an important programme on TV. (Ladies, please don't send in your protests. I now know the error of my ways and am reformed – I have Sky+ – I can pause the TV whilst she talks.)

When I saw her next, Rebekah wondered what programme could be so important that I couldn't talk to her, and I explained that it was about funerals. She seemed inexplicably baffled and more than a little offended by that answer so I had to expand. I told her that as a sideline, I have a little company that supplies white doves for funerals. The birds are released after the ceremony at the graveside.

Rebekah seemed incredulous so I carried on – the doves are actually homing pigeons that return to my mate, Martin's, dovecote in between their tasks. I think she thought I was pulling her leg, so I fished out my business card to show her – Doves International. This was the point at which she said, 'Doves at funerals that are really pigeons that fly home? Do you also have a Robin Reliant and a partner called Rodney?' I didn't take offence – I consider Del Boy to have been quite an entrepreneur.

The truth is, I've done all sorts of things in my time to help pay the bills. I've worked with a removals company when they needed an extra hand shifting pianos. I certainly felt I'd earned my wage at the end of those days. I once remember having to manoeuvre a piano up five flights of stairs; it is one of my regular prayers that I never have to do that again. There are techniques that make moving furniture much easier, but at the end of the day a piano is a piano and should be kept at ground level.

I used to sell hot tubs, too; together with a couple of mates, I had a little yard in our village and we sold, delivered and fitted them. I've also always used my magic skills to do kids' parties locally, I'm an eBay master, and I've managed to appear in a couple of TV adverts.

I auditioned for a part in a Müller Rice advert – very excited because it meant travelling to South Africa – but I lost out to the guy who played layabout, Keith Miller, in *EastEnders*. He wasn't quite so ill-kempt back then it's important to add. Another time, I was auditioning for the part of a burglar in an insurance advert, but the producer decided that I looked too 'nice' so I got cast as a delivery man instead. I wasn't quite sure what I made of being 'too nice', but went with it – it was all work.

I've done all manner of things, but my passion remains

spreading the Good News. I want to find as many ways as I can to get the News out there. I love performing, using tricks and escapology to demonstrate God's message. I'm passionate about *Sorted*, our men's magazine, and the opportunities it's providing to introduce blokes to God in a non-threatening or cringe-worthy way. These things are what I believe I have been called to do – to keep finding new ways to communicate God's love in a way that people understand.

But this doesn't mean that it's *all* I have to do. There have been times when I have needed to find other bits of work; times when I have struggled to pay the bills. I don't just get the glory jobs; I've had to grit my teeth and get on with far less appealing tasks, too. Speaking on behalf of God is an honour that I treasure but it doesn't mean that I don't have to earn my keep.

It's easy to think that, as Christians, we should have a smooth ride – we're working for the King, we're on Kingdom business, we have a higher calling – surely we shouldn't have to get our hands dirty? I don't think the Bible promises us any such thing. Even the apostle Paul – Saint Paul, father of the modern Church, author of much of the New Testament and the man who took the Good News to the nations – had a sideline making tents. He didn't just depend on God to miraculously provide money for him; he used the gifts God had given him to provide for himself.

I could get into trouble here, so let me say that I believe that God can and does provide miraculously for His people – over and over again. Indeed He has done for me. I have had cheques posted through my door when I have most needed them; I have had tax rebates that I never expected, gifts from generous friends, and anonymous contributions from people who I can never personally thank. But I also believe that God has given us the means with which to provide for ourselves. He has given us two hands, two feet and a brain with which to coordinate them, and we should use them when we need to and when we are able.

In this credit crunch era in which we live, there will be many of us who face tough times. We will lose jobs, we might struggle to find new ones and we will need to depend on God to provide. He will – the Bible tells us so. Jesus, talking to His disciples, pointed out that, just as God provides for the birds of the air and plants of the ground, so He will provide for us – we are infinitely more valuable than they are.

So let's look to our Father in Heaven to provide for our needs, let's trust Him to look after us as He has promised. But let's not turn our noses up at the ways in which He might do this and deem the solution unworthy. If Paul could sit with a needle and thread and sew for a living, then surely we can turn our hands to all manner of things.

If all else fails, you could always get a job with Trotters Independent Traders.

43

NAME DROPPING

I've had some trips in my time. I travel thousands of miles a month, often by myself. I like to have someone with me. Driving for hours on end on your own can be a killer – literally. Having someone to chat with me and keep me going is a real bonus.

At least it's a bonus most of the time, although not on the day when I was driving from the south coast to Derby with a certain Mr Christian Schneibel in the car. I was giving him a lift to a big conference where I was speaking. We managed the first couple of hours passing pleasantries and listening in companionable silence to the radio. What I didn't realise was the inner turmoil going on in my German friend's mind. My music, it seemed, was unwholesome and he was struggling sharing the same space with it.

When I realised that he was getting twitchy, I asked him to explain so that I could help in some way. He launched into an attack on the moral standards of Radio 1 – a point I couldn't really argue with. He then went on to extol the virtues of classical music, and this I *could* argue with. I'm not a complete cave man – I do appreciate a lot of classical music, but you can't tell me that all those composers were moral giants. Some of them were complete nutters whose personal lives wouldn't bear close scrutiny. Beethoven, whom my passenger was praising, had a number of affairs and treated his brother's widow and son in the most terrible way – no matter how beautiful his music may have been.

Before I had time to argue my point, however, my companion made an announcement in no more words than these – 'Right, I sleep now.' He then leant over, turned the radio off and the heating up before reclining his seat, closing his eyes and sleeping for the next three hours. I was more than a little shocked.

I barely knew this man, yet here he was being rude about my choice of radio channel, curt about his need for sleep, and turning the heat up and radio off without even asking in *my* car. I like to think I'm a hospitable man, but when I'm driving, the radio helps me to keep going whilst heat makes me drowsy. I felt like a taxi driver rather than someone doing this man a favour. He didn't even say thank you when we finally arrived at the conference centre. And he got a bigger room than I did.

It was an International Children's Workers Conference organised by Ishmael and his wife, Irene. We were one of two parties at the conference centre, and it was wonderful to catch up with so many old friends. As we stood in the lobby waiting to check in, I noticed a sign for the other conference – the Finnish Friends' Fellowship – saying their entrance was at the other side of the building.

I don't know if the silence had gone to my head or whether I'd been affected detrimentally by the sauna in my car, but I took it upon myself to don my best Scandinavian accent – and it's good I might say; my mum's Danish, so I've learnt from the master.

I picked up the sign to welcome my friends from the North and started prancing around the foyer making up announcements for the Finns. I thought I was very funny. Even our delegates did. They thought it even funnier when two ladies with white blonde hair walked in and asked me to guide them to their room. I didn't know how to explain myself, so I went to the desk, asked the girls there for my Finnish Friends' room number, then picked up their bags and showed them the way. I was a little quieter on my return.

Keen to get over the embarrassments of earlier, I was looking forward to the evening when we were going to a local curry house, minus a certain Herr Schneibel. Now, curry is something I get passionate about. I just love my hot food. I don't have a favourite dish – I just like it hot and full of flavour. There is something wonderful about the aromas that float out of an Indian restaurant and as we got closer, I felt my spirits lift; it was like coming home – even though I'd never been to this restaurant before.

It was even more like home when, after we had all taken our seats and looked at the menu, the waiter came up with his pad and pen and said, 'Pint of cobra and a Chicken Vindaloo for you, Steve?' It was Shah, my old mate from Tandoori Nights in Rustington. I'd been a regular there for years and he'd remembered me. He then turned to Ishy and Irene and remembered that Irene always preferred red wine. How fantastic. It's a little thing, really, but it felt great to have been remembered; awesome that he knew our names – it made us feel amazing.

Names are funny things. Actually, they can be very funny. I was listening on the radio the other day to a phone-in about unfortunate names – Kylie Wylie, Candy Kane and Stan Tup were just some of the names unthinking parents had given to their children. But our names are important – they tell people who we are. When we got married, Rebekah spent days writing to banks, government bodies and anyone else who might need to know that her name had changed. It was a drag, but part of her loved it – her name is a mark of our relationship.

Most of all, names are personal – I loved it that the waiter remembered my name. It turned me from a customer into a friend. I try really hard to remember people's names; it means such a lot to someone to know that you can bring to mind what they're called. I embarrass my kids in the supermarket by reading the checkout assistants' badges and referring to them by name, but I want them to know that they are more than someone who is paid to serve me – I want to acknowledge them as individuals.

It can be easy to lose track of the people we meet – particularly when we're reaching out to those outside the Church. People can become projects – those we're trying to convert; those we want to help; even those we're meaning to serve. Our outreach can become the focus instead of the people we're meeting.

It shouldn't be this way. When Jesus walked on earth, He

spoke to huge crowds but He connected with individuals – He gave them time, and showed them that they were people in their own right. He met the woman at the well and let her know that He knew everything about her and still loved her, and He sat down and ate a meal with Zaccheus, the hated tax collector. When He met Mary in the Garden of Gethsemane, crying because she thought He was dead, He called her by name and changed her world forever.

The personal touch matters – it's the difference between duty and love. Let's make sure that we value the people we meet, that we let them know that we're interested in them; their past, their present and their future. Let's invest some real time in getting to know them and show them the respect they deserve.

It's what Jesus did.

44

WOOD YOU BELIEVE IT?

My mum is one of my greatest fans. When she first met Rebekah, they sat on the sofa and, totally predictably, within ten minutes, she had mentioned what a wonderful reader I was at school, that I had sat my 'O' level English a year early and was deputy head boy although really, of course, I should have been head boy. Rebekah barely contained her snorts of laughter as my dear mother's pride flowed like a river from her. I went and made a cup of tea and didn't resurface until the conversation had changed.

School was a bit of a mixed bag for me – there were some subjects that I loved and English was amongst them. It started way back at primary school and all because of the lovely Miss Humphreys. She was truly inspirational and the best teacher in our school. Because of her I could, and still can, immerse myself in a book and block out the rest of the world, and I discovered I could often express myself more clearly through the written word than the spoken.

But back at secondary school, there were other subjects where my teachers shook their heads and despaired of me. Woodwork was one of them. It didn't seem to matter what was asked of me, I got it wrong. I would use nails instead of screws and when my teacher asked me for a spanner, I brought a screwdriver. We were asked to design a small wooden box to store treasures in; mine looked as though it had travelled half-way around the world and been through the digestive tracts of several large animals and then, when you took the lid off, it fell apart.

The teachers were a pretty mixed bag, too, of wonderful eccentrics – I can't remember Mr Fry without the words 'YOU BOY' echoing through my ears one more time. Mr Vingo was head of PE, and was just like the Brian Conley character in *The Grimleys*. He had a certain John Wayne gait and would often bellow, 'Don't kick the basketball!' across our sports hall.

I still smile remembering chemistry lessons, playing Blockbusters rather than doing chemical experiments, and squirm as I remember how off-putting it was trying to do any work once while Mr Cornick stood, one leg up on a chair with his flies undone. His catchphrase was, 'Er, no, we don't do that', and he produced worksheets on his archaic typewriter with a wpm rate that barely reached double digits. An old-style teacher, he had named his slipper *Mr Dunlop* and his cane *Mr Whippy*. I never enjoyed an ice cream in quite the same way ever again.

Mr Stewart in metalwork was nicknamed Captain Caveman, due to a shockingly bushy beard and eyebrows. He guaranteed his place in the Kingsleigh School hall of fame the day he set light to his jacket when he put his pipe in his pocket – something 'Cavey' never did.

A somewhat happier memory is Mr Bosanko – my wonderful music teacher. I could never forget his tight perm, or the pride he took in his brand new estate car, which, two years after he bought it, still had the plastic covers on the seats. He gave me a love of brass instruments and was a real encouragement to me as a member of the school band. What a character. We all thought he was great.

It was somewhat different, however, with Mr Bray. He, most definitely, was not my biggest fan. To be fair, I wasn't his. Out of earshot we called him 'Big Bird'. He had a tiny little head and his body just seemed to grow like a pyramid out beneath it. Like a wannabe chemist, he never went anywhere without his white lab coat and if I had a pound for every time he stroked a sanded piece of wood and said, 'It's as smooth as a baby's bottom and twice as clean', I'd be considerably better off.

But I was still rubbish at woodwork. On one particularly memorable occasion, I'd decided to ingratiate myself with Mr Bray and popped into the workshop at lunchtime to ask if there was anything I could do to help. He looked sceptical but motioned to a large, beautiful, antique mahogany box and asked me to take it apart. Keen to be helpful, I set to work whilst he went off for a smoke.

I found the sharpest chisel I could, and the largest hammer, and began to chip away at the batons that held the box together. Initially I was irritated by the way the screws got in the way of my chisel, until I realised that had I just unscrewed them, the box would have come apart. It dawned on me that there may have been a better way of fulfilling this task at the precise moment Mr Bray came back to check my progress.

Furious, only begins to describe him. He was incandescent and went many different shades of red. Having sworn at me in language I shan't repeat, he went on to point out that I had ruined his box, ruined his chisel and above all else, committed the ultimate crime of using a hammer instead of a mallet.

He waved the hammer at my head and asked me whether it would hurt if he hit me with it. Confused, I replied that of course it would, but that it would hurt just as much if he hit me with a mallet. That was a mistake. 'Yes sir, no sir' would have fit the bill at that point. Back chat was asking for it no matter how well intended it was. Mr Bray then launched into a full-on tirade about how stupid I was, how I would never amount to anything, would never achieve anything and would be a waste of space for the rest of my life.

He did calm down eventually, but it took a few days. To give him his dues, I am still rubbish at woodwork and have had more DIY disasters than I like to admit. In our house, DIY stands for 'Destroy It Yourself'. But I have achieved many things. I am not a complete waste of space and I have made something of myself through God.

I should think there are many of us who, at some point or other, have had a Mr Bray moment. It may not have been a teacher – it may have been the bully at school, our elder brother or sister, maybe even our own parents. It might have been our boss at work. Perhaps we've been told we're ugly, or stupid, fat or difficult. We get told these things in all kinds of situations and it can be hard to let go of them. It's much easier to believe the bad things that people say about us than the good.

But the truth is we don't have to be what other people say we are. We have an identity in Christ – we are children of the King and anyone who says differently is plain wrong. We need to shake off the labels that people give us, and refuse to fulfil their gloomy prophecies; we get to choose where we will go with our lives and what we will be. We can choose to live them with God.

God tells us in Isaiah that we are *'precious and honoured in His sight'*, and in Psalms He tells us that *'we are fearfully and wonderfully made'*. Paul, in his letter to the Philippians, reminds us that we can do *'all things through Him that strengthens us'*. God has given each one of us extraordinary gifts – be they to dangle upside down and escape from a strait jacket or to lend a compassionate ear to someone who needs to talk. And if we'll only allow Him, He'll lead us to use our gifts in situations more remarkable than we could ever have imagined.

Life with God is an incredible adventure. Through it all, His love will surround us, and whatever comes our way, He will never leave our sides. There is no one whose authority is greater than God's, so stand firm in His promises and live your life to the max.

Whatever you do, don't let the Big Bird get you down.

Also by Steve Legg

Making Friends – Evangelism the Easy Way
Man, Myth or Maybe More?
Big Questions
The A-Z of Evangelism
Firm Foundations
The A-Z of Christmas
The Chancer

By Steve Legg
and Alexa Tewkesbury

It's a Boy!
Lions, Whales and Thrilling Tales
The Lying Tree
cyberSky

Sorted

The UK's Number One Christian Magazine For Men

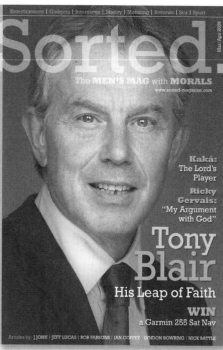

Reasons to Subscribe

- Special subscriber-only offers
- Top columnists
- Great sports pages
- Become part of the Christian publishing world's fastest growing success story
- Qualify to grab copies of our sister paper, *The Son*, at reduced rates and win the lost
- Receive every bi-monthly issue before it hits the shops
- More free magazines sent into jails in the UK and to death row prisoners in Africa
- Hundreds more copies can be sent overseas to support and encourage members of the armed forces

" What an innovative and creative magazine. New, fresh and insightful. I recommend it unreservedly. **"** J.JOHN